Reflections from the former Torture & Trauma Counselling Team on Christmas Island

'Chris's memoir is an important piece integrating her story into history to ensure that these experiences and those accountable are not conveniently erased through the turnover of staff and the changing of governments. This is a rare offering from a woman who shares intimately first-hand accounts of stories that are deliberately kept out of mainstream Australian media. In our four-room demountable counselling building, situated at the back of the local community hospital, Chris had her office at one end and I was at the other end. Frequently I would hear Chris's infectious laugh, it's reassuring and joyful sound reverberating around our little building and out would come Chris with a woman/man/child/whole family and an interpreter who couldn't stop smiling despite the tear streaks reflecting the horrors they may have been sharing a moment before.

I recall Chris, when meeting with anyone, whether they be a Serco guard, an immigration officer, an important government figure or a person seeking asylum, had this way of extending a warmth that would simply envelope the person *but* as equally warm as Chris is she is also unapologetic in holding her ethics and intentions for all the world to see and take heed – nothing was to be tolerated that impinged on another person's rights and dignity.

It was Chris's courage and vast knowledge and wisdom that kept our little counselling team afloat amongst the political storms that rolled and washed over Christmas Island. I am truly grateful to Chris who constantly and consistently offered herself as the buffer, taking on the systemic and political madness to give us a small space so that we could get on with the most important work – responding to people facing the harm of multiple traumas and injustice.'

– Poh Lin Lee

'The three years spent working in the Torture and Trauma counselling team on Christmas Island were life changing. It was an absolute privilege to meet and work with such courageous people, to be trusted with their stories and share some of their journey. The challenges of working against such a toxic

and damaging system were overwhelming at times and would not have been possible without the incredible support and leadership of Chris, along with Poh, Jan and Leigh. A never-ending passion for social justice and belief in upholding dignity, as well as a sense of humour kept the team strong.'

– Petrina Yates

'I spent a year and three months on the idyllic and confronting Christmas Island. During that time I worked in Chris's small team of Torture and Trauma Counsellors, an experience that shaped my life. We delivered our work trapped between the forces of government powers and our professional ethics. Our belief in social justice and human rights clashed with bureaucratic idiocies. In that climate of ideological and physical isolation we needed each other's support, trust and love to stay sane. We shared some intimate parts of our lives with each other which formed rare bonds steeled by all our experiences.'

– Jan Wetzel

'Working in Christine's therapy team on Christmas Island, I gained insight into the complexities of Australian immigration detention and the multiple layers of trauma experienced by asylum seekers along with their extraordinary strengths. A key goal of therapy with trauma survivors is to help clients gain a sense of safety and control. It was rare on Christmas Island, however, to work with individuals who could sustain a meaningful sense of safety and stability, given they were so focused on surviving, i.e. surviving prolonged detention and detention trauma. In a context where 'border security' conflicted heavily with human rights and trauma recovery, strong client advocacy became just as central in our work as providing therapy. Although our dedicated team worked tirelessly to address complex ethical dilemmas, the work increasingly felt like collusion with an inherently harmful system. In what felt like an impossible yet privileged choice to make, we decided as a team to leave the island. The extraordinary individuals I worked with on Christmas Island continue to inspire me and my work to this day.'

– Leigh Johnston

Dignity in a Teacup

True stories of courage and sacrifice from Christmas Island

CHRISTINE CUMMINS

ARCADIA

First published 2019 by ARCADIA
the general books' imprint of
Australian Scholarly Publishing Pty Ltd
7 Lt Lothian St Nth, North Melbourne, Vic 3051
Tel: 03 9329 6963 / Fax: 03 9329 5452
enquiry@scholarly.info / www.scholarly.info

ISBN 978-1-925801-56-9

Cover: Photography by Liz Graco

Cover design: Amelia Walker

For Isabella & Omid

Contents

Map

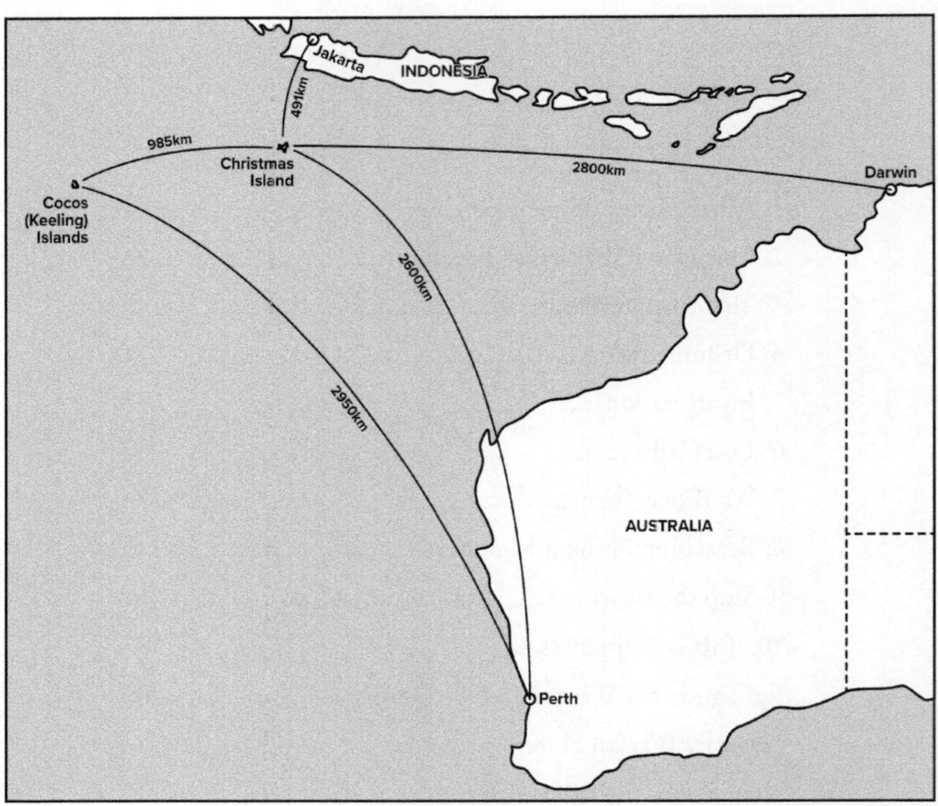

Christmas Island is located in the Indian Ocean 2,623 kilometres north-west of Perth. It is 19 kilometres long and 14 kilometres wide and has an area of 137.4 square kilometres. The island became an Australian Territory in 1958 prior to this it had been administered as a British possession by the Colony of Singapore, and had, from the middle of the nineteenth century, been administered by British Governors in Ceylon or Singapore under the Straits Settlements. Christmas and the Cocos (Keeling) Islands are known as the Indian Ocean Territories and administered by the Department of Infrastructure and Regional Development

Author's note

I have wrestled over my decision to use the stories of the people I counselled. When I invited each person into the counselling room it was an invitation to trust in me, to share their grief, anger, sorrow, horror, joy, pain, love and fear in a space offering safety and respect and I have never intended to betray that trust. The more I was asked about my experience on Christmas Island the more people wanted to learn, and I soon discovered that even the most informed were often ill-informed and I found myself giving melded examples of stories as explainers. These sample stories gave context to a story-line of tragedy distorted by political propaganda, I recognised my audience were often disconnected, and lacking in trust and understanding. By allowing a glimpse into the life of a refugee, their stories explain why people have been forced to flee their homelands and they speak of courage and sacrifice. When people heard these firsthand accounts they wanted to learn more and then quite wonderfully, they advocated for refugees and informed others, so I felt that I was on to something that would humanise these forgotten people. I started to wonder if I should document my experiences and share the stories of many of the people I counselled, to enable the broader community greater insight into the magnitude of the refugees strengths and suffering. So, I was challenged by an ethical dilemma of my own making and sort advice and counsel. I tossed and turned in my sleep at night but in the end I decided the stories are too important not to share. I was lucky to have the blessing of some of the people I write about, some people were adamant I should do whatever I can to make their voices heard. Where I could, I sort permission to share however; there are many people I was unable to find. I have altered names and key identifiers in an effort to protect the privacy of these incredible people and I hope that my motivation for sharing is clear. People seeking asylum need sanctuary but importantly, they also need to be heard and understood.

Preface

He was a tall man probably six foot four; it struck me that he carried a physical burden exhausting his limbs as he sank deep into the arm chair his knees raised up to his chest rapidly disempowering him, as if he were a small boy in a grown-ups' chair. His story was both intriguing and heartbreaking. As the lover of stories my curiosity never wavers whilst Peter recounted his life to date I felt as I always have, an innate need to offer comfort, practical support and to nurture. I listened intently all the while mapping how I would help this man and ease some of the burden. He described a deep faith that led him into a catholic seminary in Jaffna in the far north of Sri Lanka and how in 1990 he was one of the hundreds of thousands of Tamil people to become displaced when the civil war conflict intensified. The displacement forced him to leave theological studies but he was encouraged by a senior priest to continue a life of dedication working in the field of social justice.

In 1995 he started to work as a project officer for a local Non-Government Organisation (NGO), the Tamil Rehabilitation Organisation, his eyes became alive when he talked about his work making it was clear to me that he had found his passion through helping others. He supervised development workers on water projects, building wells and facilitating health and education programs, he had to travel and live in different areas depending on the project and in 2008 found himself working in the Mullaitivu district. It was here that Peter witnessed the massacres. By January 2009 the Sri Lankan army commanded all international NGO's to leave the area, but they deliberately held the local NGO's in the area. The workers were forced to witness the deaths and to bury the dead. It was burying the children and babies that had an agonising effect on Peter.

He couldn't erase the memory from his mind. He had witnessed hungry dogs eating dead bodies and the direct shelling of a line of children innocently waiting for a ration of milk powder. It was 2010 when we met, Peter was forty-four years old and a father of three young daughters he had left behind in Sri Lanka, we talked about the trauma of watching these horrors and he described the haunting sound of children crying in hunger and terror. Peter was convinced that he would never be the same after witnessing these events and that having to bury so many people had permanently changed him. This was undoubtedly true, but I knew change didn't have to be destructive and I hoped to show him that. Following the end of the war, the army started arresting and imprisoning the directors and senior workers from the local NGO's and Peter's name was on the list. He believed they were doing this to suppress the details of the massacres from the international community and he felt his only real option was to flee. Peter had maintained his strong faith in God and his religion and I utilised this strength in his therapy, he had already been equipped with the ability to move through his pain and I simply guided him.

* * *

When I first arrived on Christmas Island I was the fourth and final addition to a new start-up torture and trauma counselling team. I arrived in January 2010 on a sunny Saturday afternoon my eight-year-old daughter Isabella by my side. We were excited and looking forward to a fabulous adventure exploring the magical island famous for its red crab migration, it was going to be a cultural experience and I felt grateful for the opportunity to experience life on this remote Australian territory.

I began my working life as an enrolled nurse and I took this as far as I could, nursing in Saudi Arabia, spending a year as a volunteer nurse in children's homes in Sri Lanka, and working for Médecins Sans Frontières in Iran with Afghan refugees. I nursed in the remote Kimberley region of Western Australia and briefly in the Northern Territory. I went to university after the birth of my daughter and gained my degree in nursing and a post-graduate diploma in mental health nursing after completing a graduate nurse program in mental health with Bendigo Health in regional Victoria. Mental health became a passion, I was able to advocate and care for people so marginalised that society often remains frightened and confused by their suffering and the bonus is, it's rewarding work.

After spending a few years working in community case management, crisis assessment and with a primary mental health team I had started to develop my interest and skills in trauma focussed therapies. Trauma-Informed practice is a strengths-based framework grounded in an understanding of the impact of trauma, emphasising physical, psychological, and emotional safety for the client. It's essential to rebuild a sense of control and empowerment for traumatised people, this is challenging and draws on a multitude of tools in the therapist toolkit. I find that it is important to be accepting of the individuals own beliefs and I seek to discover what those belief systems are early in the therapy to help guide the direction. For example, I look at the social, emotional and spiritual components of the individual human experience because I find this sometimes leads to instilling hope. I don't have to share the same beliefs but I do respect and acknowledge each client and use this as my starting point.

When I saw the advertisement for a position on Christmas Island I grabbed the opportunity to work with the same people groups I had experienced in my foreign-aid work and to further develop my trauma therapy skills. It wasn't long before I found that being a torture and trauma counsellor received a fairly standard reaction when someone asked what I did for a living, they were usually intrigued and asked how and why I chose the field. I recognised that knowing *how* to do the job and knowing *why* I did the job were two very different things. The work itself could be bloody hard, I offered people the opportunity to share their story and be heard. For many people this was their first experience of being listened too, listening can be very powerful. I found that the hardest stories, the nightmare experiences can be dealt with when someone genuinely cares and listens, so that's what I did.

The *why* I did it unfolds here in this memoir. I met far too many people to ignore their stories, and I watched on as those in power turned the majority of Australians into refugee and asylum seeker doubters or even haters. I am still astonished by the access I was granted to the mechanisms of the Department of Immigration and to the immigration detention facilities on Christmas Island. This permitted access invited my presence during a significant period in our nation's history and it allowed me to bear witness to policy changes that I believe future generations will view as nothing short of shameful. I recognise that people seeking asylum are muted from discussion, their stories are not heard because the debates rage with greater force when the public and policy makers remain disconnected and desperation remains voiceless. It is with this recognition that I share some of the experiences of the people I journeyed with for five years; it's time to hear their voices too.

From Top

Flying Fish Cove Christmas Island, a view from the Territory Park lookout, 2008. The cove is the location of the jetty where all boat arrivals stepped foot off the boats. DIAC images

A view from Jack's Hill. The Christmas Island Immigration Detention Centre at the North West Point of the island referred to as NWP, 2011. DIAC images

The electrified fortified fencing surrounding the Immigration Detention Centre, 2015. Photograph by David Stanley

From Top

Entrance to the Christmas Island Immigration Detention Centre, 2008. DIAC images

A boat arrival being escorted by Customs officers to the jetty, 7 December 2008. DIAC images

The Torture and Trauma Counseling team 2013/2014. L to r: Poh Lin Lee, Jan Wetzel, Christine Cummins, and Petrina Yates

Chapter 1

What Makes People Flee

Refugees are not pawns on the chessboard of humanity. They are children, women and men who leave or who are forced to leave their homes for various reasons, who share a legitimate desire for knowing and having, but above all for being.

Pope Francis

The Kumar family, Sri Lanka

They were broken people when we met, each face staring blankly, they sat opposite me the three of them on a small couch, their ten-year-old daughter Sylvia sandwiched between her parents, protected and loved. Thirty-three-year-old Lavinia softly cried as she attempted to speak, her husband Joseph remained protective and strong, he knew Lavinia needed to share their story and he would let her do this through the tears. I leant forward to offer a box of tissues and found Lavina's hand on mine in an instant. She needed me to feel her wretched sadness as if the grief could be transferred through touch, I held her hand as she shared her story and her grief. This intimate exchange drew me into the sharing of this painful story and whilst Lavina's tears fell, Sylvia's silent resolve nearly broke my heart.

They had owned a small textile business in Kilinochchi in the far north of the country and had grown used to the madness of war, the shelling, the noise, the constant fear and destruction. In the midst of it they tried to live a purposeful life and as devoted Catholics they used their faith to sustain them. In January 2009 the family were among the many thousands of Tamils who became displaced, the conflict had escalated and they found themselves in Mullaitivu, the place of the final battle. Along with thousands of other people the Kumar's had been herded into a camp in the safe zone with their three young children, Sylvia who was nine, Mary aged seven and three-year-old Michael.

On the Fifteenth of April 2009 the Sri Lankan military shelled the camp repeatedly; the Kumar's described the scene as chaotic people running in every direction desperately trying to find a way out. The family were caught in the middle of this intense conflict and watched helplessly as their youngest children Mary and Michael were hit and killed by the shelling. Lavinia's tears fell and her shoulders heaved as she described how they were forced to flee leaving the bodies of their children lying alongside countless others, later to be buried in a mass grave.

Lavinia sustained serious abdominal wounds and needed emergency surgery while Joseph had severe wounds to his right arm. Their memory of this is blurred however they were told that they were initially taken to the Vavuniya hospital, then over the course of six weeks Lavinia and Joseph were sent to different hospitals to have surgery while little Sylvia stayed by her mother's side the entire time. Eventually the family was reunited in a camp hospital where they were offered assistance by the husband of another patient, he offered to help smuggle them out and away from the camp. This complete stranger bribed two army officers and arranged for them to go into hiding in Colombo while false passports were arranged, they sold Lavinia's jewellery to fund their escape.

At this point of the sharing Joseph joined in, with a deep controlled voice he was a commanding presence, this was also an opportune time to give Lavinia a break and I could see she was grateful to him. He told me about the day an army officer came to the safe house conducting a routine search in the area. They were alerted to the sound of someone coming into the house when they were in the bedroom, with nowhere to run they quickly hid under a bed together. Holding their breath, they watched the black boots of a soldier step into the room. Expecting to be discovered at any moment they watched the soldier's feet move around the room and as were surprised to hear the small television switched on, the mattress above sank with his weight as he sat on the bed and watched the cricket for forty-five minutes. When the match was over he simply got off the bed, turned the television off and walked out the door, Joseph said that he always watches cricket with a smile saying *it saved our lives!*

After two weeks in the safe house they received their passports and tickets to fly to India, but at the airport they were separated and interrogated individually, including young Sylvia. Joseph was clearly angered by the fact his little girl had been taken and questioned however the outcome was good when they were eventually allowed to board the plane. They stayed in India for six months where they regularly attended a Catholic church and it was at this church that they were approached by a man offering assistance to get them to Australia. Lavinia told me they were offered a cheap deal after telling the man of the death of their children, she said the man had felt so sorry for them and accepted payment for just one fare to cover the three of them. They travelled by boat from Tamil Nadu in India until they were found by an Australian Customs boat near Christmas Island. They had spent twenty-four days at sea the final three days without food or water.

The greatest heartbreak for this family was the graphic memory they each shared of Mary and Michael's bodies left with all the other victims of the massacre. Their grief was so immense, so raw, that while they had mended physically from the wounds, the sadness was overwhelming stunting any hope of healing. I learnt very early on, that if someone presents with a strong faith or spirituality I could use it as a pathway to healing. The Kumar's

Catholic faith had held them together through the most traumatic times and was the key to their healing. I recognised the importance a Catholic memorial service would have for this family and organised one to be held at the local church and a second one in the detention centre where many more Tamils could attend. The priest was one of the many volunteer priests that arrived on the island for a month at a time to provide pastoral care to the predominantly Catholic Tamil asylum seekers, he was very respectful of their need to mourn with a ritual that honoured their culture. The Kumar's had a photo of Mary and Michael and I copied this onto a memorial card and an interpreter kindly lent me a Tamil prayer book to help source an appropriate prayer. Each person who attended was given the memorial card and it was this small gesture that was so very important to Lavinia because it was how things would have been done at home. For the Kumar's the memorial was an opportunity to mourn, to reflect on the great sadness they had endured and to open a pathway to healing, however I can still hear the primal keening of Lavinia when I allow myself to reflect on this ceremony because it was honestly gut wrenching.

After the memorial services I started to prepare individual sessions for each member of the family, wanting to guide each of them through their grief and trauma or so I planned. When the family failed to attend the next appointment, I was told they had been transferred to the Darwin immigration facility which was not unusual, particularly as Lavinia still needed surgical follow-up for her war wounds and medical transfers at the time were often sent to Darwin. I wanted to make sure this loving family did not fall through the cracks, and miss out on receiving the care they needed and I referred the family through to the torture and trauma counselling service in Darwin. I remember wondering why I was being given the run around when trying to discuss their referral with the detention centre medical staff in Darwin, they were being non-committal and avoidant. The reason became abundantly clear after I was eventually told in confidence that the Kumar's had been refused asylum and forcibly deported to Sri Lanka. I was really distressed by this news and unable to verify this information due to the Department of Immigration citing privacy regulations, I have always wondered what became of them. I'm left with an enduring memory of Sylvia's stunned eyes, Lavinia's raw grief and Joseph's stoic love and protection for his family. I also kept the memorial card as a reminder of the importance of faith and personal courage and of the need to ensure people can heal with dignity.

Somali poet Warsan Shire wrote *no one puts their children in a boat unless the water is safer than the land*. This was a fact I grew to understand intimately. Fear and love make people flee, spurred on by a natural instinct to survive and to protect loved ones. People seeking asylum are no different to you and I, each one of us would do whatever it takes to survive and protect yet I still feel compelled to write this obvious fact. It appears the fear and love experienced in countries such as Somalia or Syria is not always accepted as of equal value to the fear and love experienced in Australia and the developed world.

The simplest way to explain why people are forced to flee their homes to seek asylum is with a brief summary of the facts and figures, firstly people become displaced, meaning they run away from home. This is often within their country of origin, when safety cannot be found, they then cross a border seeking asylum. In 2017 the United Nations estimated 68.5 million people identified as either displaced, seeking asylum or recognised as refugees. The same data shows that children made up approximately 52 per cent of the refugee population, including 173,800 unaccompanied or separated children.

To be recognised as a refugee people are required to register with the United Nations High Commission for Refugees (UNHCR) to lodge a formal claim for asylum. The numbers of people accessing this process is almost insignificant because it's impossible and impractical for millions, for the vast majority of people there is little or no access to the UNHCR to allow any form of registration and assessment of refugee status. In 2011 only eleven percent of the world's asylum claims were registered. Worldwide the total number of refugees has increased significantly and consistently over a seven-year period starting from 10.4 million at the end of 2011 reaching an estimated 25.3 million in 2017. Each registered claim has to be assessed but this process can take years and only after the person is found to meet the criteria that they will be declared a refugee. People are forced to seek asylum for a number of reasons, but to meet the criteria for refugee status there are five criteria under the *United Nations Convention Relating to the Status of Refugees* established in 1951. Commonly referred to as the *Refugee Convention* the document defines a refugee as someone who 'owing to a well-founded fear of being persecuted for reasons of race, religion, nationality, membership of a particular social group or political opinion, is outside the country of his nationality, and is unable to, or owing to such fear, is unwilling to avail himself of the protection of that country.'[1]

The UNHCR stresses that a person who has a well-founded fear of persecution should be viewed as a refugee and not be labelled an 'illegal immigrant' as the very nature of persecution means that their only means of escape may be by illegal entry and with the use of false documentation. Asylum seekers irrespective of their mode of arrival, like others that arrive in Australia without a valid visa, are classified by Australian law to be 'unlawful non-citizens'. However, the term 'unlawful' does not mean that asylum seekers have committed a criminal offence, there is no offence under Australian law that criminalises the act of arriving in Australia or the seeking of asylum without a valid visa.[2] It is both disturbing and exasperating that our current government leaders insist on the use of the word 'illegal', people are not breaking laws looking for an adventure; they are accessing their human right to flee danger and to seek safety.

When people are recognised as refugees the UN may offer shelter in a registered camp however there is no obligation to offer resettlement, the UN is a global entity not a transformative reformation and it certainly can't deliver miracles. Another factor to acknowledge is the demand for resettlement that far exceeds supply. It takes about five years to get on the resettlement list and adding to grim statistics is the fact that less than one percent of the world's refugees may be resettled in any given year. Yes, that's right, one percent. The latest statistics show that just 189,300 refugees were granted resettlement with UNHCR assistance during 2016 and that's a significant increase from other years. (3) And then there is the issue of worthiness applied to asylum seekers and refugees, with many people believing a person with refugee status has more credibility than a person seeking asylum. Given the fact that registration is unavailable to millions this argument does not make sense. So too is the commonly held view that asylum seekers, particularly those who arrive by boat are jumping the queue and taking the place of a more deserving refugee awaiting resettlement in a refugee camp; in reality that orderly queue does not exist. This ensures people do what people will always do, they grab whatever opportunity they can in a fight for survival.

The imagery of survival was on regular display throughout 2015 with the world media broadcasting constant footage of desperate people seeking refuge in Europe. While overloaded boats crossed the Mediterranean Sea onto the coast of Turkey, Greece and Italy the media delivered a heartbreaking image of three-year-old Aylan Kurdi's body washed up on a Turkish beach. This single image humanised a global response to the plight of ordinary people forced to flee their homes, but the changed opinions didn't last. The enormity of the dilemma has overwhelmed us because it's easier to process the problem with detachment and safe distance. While the UN estimates around one million asylum seekers and refugees arrived in Europe in 2015 we often chose to disregard the crisis, but remember that beautiful little boy, his name was Aylan.

Survival can be a huge struggle, it is common for refugees to be forced to wait in countries such as Indonesia, Pakistan, Kenya and Lebanon for ten years or more where they are often detained by corrupt authorities demanding money for their release. These countries are not signatories to the Refugee Convention however they have the largest number of refugees, with

1.6 million refugees living in Pakistan and 1.2 million in Lebanon because they border countries in conflict. The majority of people seeking asylum are forced to flee over the closest border where they shelter in a form of limbo, always waiting to head back home where they truly wish to be. The life of a refugee or asylum seeker is one of constant fear and uncertainty, people are denied basic human rights such as access to healthcare, the right to work and the right to education. The incidents of rape and of woman and young girls being forced into the sex trade are high, as too is the disappearance and murder of many. I heard many accounts of imprisonment and beatings by Indonesian military and police, I learnt of detention centres on small Indonesian islands where people are detained for months or years because they don't have the money to buy their way out. With heartache and fury women spoke of being forced into prostitution to protect their children and they regularly described their desperate vulnerability in foreign lands.

Australian governments both past and present have led us to believe we are fulfilling our global duty to the issue of refugee resettlement by responding in a responsible and humane manner. Australia's refugee resettlement program was ranked second in the world in 2013, behind only the US and marginally ahead of Canada. These three countries hosted ninety percent of resettled refugees in 2013 making us sound incredibly generous and humanitarian until it's understood the resettled refugees account for less than four percent of recognised refugees. In reality, Australia's response is despairingly minimal and actually reducing at a time of global crisis.

Our refugee intake has always been negligible, accepting an average of six thousand people each year is not globally responsive. In June 2012 Prime Minister Gillard announced the government would establish an expert advisory panel to consider options for 'the best way forward for our nation in dealing with asylum seeker issues'. The expert panel recommended the government increase Australia's annual quota to twenty thousand including people arriving by boat with the aim to increase our intake to twenty-seven thousand within five years. However, this increase applied to just one annual intake and was promptly reduced back to just six thousand. I'm obviously disgruntled with our government's dismal response to our legal, ethical and moral duty to assist people seeking asylum. I'm also disturbed by the continuous morally corrupt use of desperate people for political gain but I refuse to despair, I know true leadership in the future can choose to change this response, I only need to look at Canada's Prime Minister Justin Trudeau to let my heart flutter. My motive for sharing is a simple one, I hope to provide insight into the lives of ordinary people seeking asylum and to honour the hundreds of men, women and children I counselled over a five-year period, I have not altered their stories, just the names and specific identifiers in an effort to protect. I share these stories because these are true narratives of real people who often experienced insurmountable pain and sorrow, people who deserve our protection and compassion with open hearts and who also deserve to have their cultural identity respected. Interspersed within all of my client's anguish and grief I consistently heard Warsan Shire's words *I want to go home, but home is the mouth of a shark, home is the barrel of the gun, and no one would leave home unless home chased you to the shore.*

I remember my first clients very well, mostly Sri Lankan Tamils who had fled their country at the end of the thirty-year civil war. Each person offered up graphic narratives of the 'final massacres' of the last months of the war. Every Tamil who presented to me was severely traumatised by years of loss, grief, displacement and the burden aligned with living life without a sense of safety. The final months of the war created estimates of three-hundred thousand displaced people, thousands herded en masse into camps against their will. Many of the asylum seekers I spoke to referred to these camps as concentration camps. Within the camps the Sri Lankan military ensured that rations were frugal and that all access to medical care was limited, everyone was treated with the same level of degradation, with no exemptions for the young, pregnant or aged. It was in these immense camps that the massacres occurred with deliberate and repeated shelling of civilians by the Sri Lankan forces to finally end the Tamil uprising by the *Liberation Tigers of Tamil Eelam* known as the LTTE or the Tamil Tigers.

The UN agencies, aid organisations and international press were forced out of the region and access to international monitors was denied. What I discovered, after listening to hundreds of individual accounts of great sadness, fear and horror was that immense injustice had been allowed and that the end of the civil war was a huge tragedy. The world watched and no one prevented the massacres, our own government and other governing bodies of the western world had known of the misery of this final battle in May 2009 and had allowed it by inactivity. I also found that the Sri Lankan government still held and most probably still hold, Tamil civilians in jungle camps where practices of torture are common. I learnt that freedom has not been granted to many men and women who remain imprisoned in Sri Lanka due to an affiliation, alleged or proven, with the Tamil Tigers. There is very little peace for a Tamil in Sri Lanka and yet this is often considered as their own fault for daring to challenge the dominant Sinhalese Sri Lankan government. It is nearly ten years after the official end of the civil war and atrocities are still occurring to Tamil civilians on a daily basis.

To understand the suffering I have learnt so much about it's worth knowing a little of the Battle of Mullaitivu because this was deemed the official end of the civil war between the Sri Lankan military and the LTTE. The town of Mullaitivu was the last stronghold of the LTTE the government troops had entered the town in January 2009 and were consolidating their positions, leaflets had been dropped over the town by the Sri Lanka Air Force urging civilians to come to government controlled Safe Zones. The government also suspended all civil administration work on the twenty-third January to allow public servants to leave the area. The army had allowed a thirty-two kilometre 'safe area' inside the war zone for civilians to exit, independent aid agencies report about 230,000 civilians were inside the war zone around the northern city.[4] According to the Sri Lankan government the purpose of the Safe Zone was to allow the trapped civilians to cross into territory controlled by the military however very few civilians actually crossed into the military territory, the Sri Lankan military along with UN and human rights organisations accused the Tamil Tigers of preventing the civilians from leaving. The fighting between the military and the Tamil Tigers continued and on 12 February 2009 the military declared a new ten square kilometre Safe Zone in the area north-west of Mullaitivu town. Over the next three months a brutal siege of the Safe Zone occurred as the military allegedly blitzed by land and air the last remnants of Tamil Tigers trapped in the Safe Zone. Satellite images of the Safe Zone published by the UN, foreign governments and scientific organisations showed heavy damage that could have only been caused by bombardment, inevitably many thousands of civilians were killed or injured. Based on credible witness evidence from aid agencies, as well as evacuated civilians numbers, the UN estimates the death toll from the final four months of the civil war from mid-January to mid-May to be from fifteen-thousand to twenty-thousand. A US State Department report suggests that the actual casualty figures were probably much higher than the UN's estimates and that significant numbers of casualties were not recorded.

As the civil war edged towards a bitter end between late April and early May the number of civilians leaving the Safe Zone turned from a trickle to a torrent and on 19 May the Sri Lankan government declared victory. After the end of the war a number of countries and human rights organisations called for an independent investigation into the final stages of the civil war. The Sri Lankan government established the 'Lessons Learnt and Reconciliation Commission' to investigate claims of war crimes however, the UN announced that the commission was deeply flawed and did not meet the international standards for effective accountability.[5] It was the victims of these atrocities we saw arriving on Christmas Island with many still in a heightened state of terror, my colleagues and I counselled hundreds of Tamils who had fled the horrors of war directly from Sri Lanka in small wooden fishing boats. Many lives were lost at sea, we will never know the actual numbers, we do know that people suffered terribly on the long journey to Christmas Island or to the Cocos (Keeling) Islands. However, each person was resolute about the fact they had no other choice but to flee their homeland seeking asylum and safety for themselves and their loved ones.

In the mid-nineties I spent twelve months living in Sri Lanka whilst the battles of war were happening in the far north and east, it didn't occur to me that I was anywhere close to danger and misery, I was naive to the reasons for the conflict and had very limited knowledge of the Tamil people, their exclusion from social rights and identity. I sat enthralled when I met some expatriate tele-communication engineers who were receiving danger money for working in Batticaloa, to me this was Hollywood style excitement. I was only confronted by the conflict when in Colombo one day a commuter bus was blown up by a suicide bomber outside a busy railway station. I remember being fascinated by the frenzied dialogue with friends that evening, some first-hand accounts of a body count far greater than the official ninety fatalities. When I saw the burnt-out bus the next day I took a photo of it, as if it were a touristic object of interest like a statute or a temple. I also souvenired a salvaged top off a landmine that I have used with unintentional callous as an interesting dinner party piece. The orphanage where I lived and worked was in a Sinhalese area one hour outside Colombo, some of the villagers had lost family members in the conflict however we didn't speak about the war and I never considered what was really happening in this beautiful island nation. I focused on the children who were mostly abandoned due to poverty and a lack of a social welfare system. Occasionally I was inconvenienced with military roadblocks, checkpoints and curfews but I remained naive to the truth of war until I sat and listened and learnt many years later.

It's a fact that working in the mental health field generally decreases the capacity to be shocked by human behaviour, which explains why bad taste black humour has evolved in the tea rooms of psychiatric units. Staff often try to outdo each other with stories of a confrontation with the bizarre and ridiculous and then there is a lot of the work that is heartbreaking and just plain sad. In the therapist's space on Christmas Island the stories I heard exposed horror, grief, fear and sadness all mixed in with a dose of hope. As gruesome as it may sound, I miss hearing the stories of pain at the moment because they often came with anticipation that I could help the client make the journey to recovery. I worked hard to develop rapport with each client, traversing their immediate suspicions and fears by offering an invitation to talk and a reason to share. Sometimes I failed to establish trust however for the vast majority, people talked and revealed and they cried and they laughed and they wrote and they painted and they sang and they started to heal.

Mathuran and Chajan

One of the many Tamils I met was twenty-one-year-old Mathuran who I counselled on a number of occasions, we were seated in my office with only one metre between us, me in the armchair and Mathuran and the interpreter near him at opposite ends of the couch. I had developed a very friendly banter with Mathuran after we had met a couple of times. He was a gregarious young guy who could look me in the eye easily and his smile was genuine, a big white teethed grin. He was always dressed in a white tee-shirt, dark green tracksuit pants and plastic flip flops, indicating he was dressed by immigration because he had arrived with nothing. He had established that I was trustworthy and so towards the end of one of our sessions he said *can I ask you to take a look at something?* He lifted his shirt to reveal a very recent surgical scar over his left side *The army came and took me,* he said *they did some operation on me and took me back to my village, what do you think?* I was horrified. He clearly had a kidney removed and he had waited for a couple of weeks before asking about it.

I can remember him giving a cheeky giggle that I interpreted as a polite way to cover his embarrassment at my startled response and his vulnerable exposure. Up until this day I had been focussing on helping him manage his frequent nightmares, this disclosure made me realise that he could not have been making any progress because I had only half the detail. Mathuran had an interesting story that was influenced by his place of birth, he had been raised in the same small coastal village famous as the birthplace of Velupillai Prabhakaran the leader of the Tamil Tigers, it was because of the strong association to Prabhakaran the village was a recognised LTTE stronghold. At the end of the war many of the villagers were captured by the military and imprisoned in a rehabilitation centre, these centres were large camps where the Sinhalese military used physical interrogation and repeated attempts at brainwashing to remove any oppositional views to the Sinhalese regime. The rehabilitation included forced labour, with men and women working long hours farming small crops, these stories of this intense rehabilitation became a common thread for many Tamils I counselled over the years.

Mathuran was rehabilitated in this manner for over twelve months, until one day he was taken for interrogation; he was accused of being an active participant in the war and received a severe beating, by then he reckoned he had taken enough of the treatment, so he fled. He was hounded through the jungle until a single gunshot to his left leg brought him down. He was taken to a hospital to have the bullet removed and his wound dressed then taken back to the rehabilitation centre. His wound healed but he was left with a limp, a few months later he was told by two officers that he was to have his leg operated on to improve his recovery. He told me he was highly suspicious of their motives however this was a directive not a humanitarian gesture and he was not in a position to decline. When he woke from surgery his leg had not been touched and he was in excruciating pain in his left side, he managed to escape because the guards were not expecting him to flee in that condition.

He made his way to his uncle's house who on seeing him knew that he had to get him out of the country immediately. The right people were contacted, clandestine plans made and within twenty-four hours Mathuran was travelling on a crowded wooden boat. The journey took twenty-seven days in horrendous conditions. Undoubtedly Mathuran would have endured immense pain on that trip, when we talked about it he knew he was very lucky to have survived the war, the surgery and the boat trip. I see him as an example of the strength of character found in someone determined to fight for life. Born during the civil war, he had never known peace, a survivor of multiple traumas he was understandably reluctant to trust anyone in a position of authority, torture and trauma counsellors included. It was only through displaying genuine interest and kindness that we established rapport with our clients, we understood anyone exposed to enduring fear, persecution and associated suffering would be reluctant to place trust in a stranger. It's also very typical in counselling that people wait out a session and leave the crucial information until the last few minutes, to create a possible escape if the disclosure of pain is too much to bare, ensuring a time shortage can allow a quick exit. Sometimes you can pre-empt it and I would book double time when I knew someone was sitting on something big and then there were people like Mathuran who completely threw me but I would somehow create extra time. Mathuran's next hurdle was learning to trust that people wanted to help him and to figure out what he was going to do with himself in a new safe world.

A vital part of our therapy was discussing the fact that survival does not represent the end of hardship, for many people the natural instinct to survive has been the only focus for so long that learning to exist without fear is frightening. This was often the case for the Tamils I counselled. Thirty years of war ensured a solid survival instinct and the ability to withstand misery, without doubt Tamils are a strong people but they also had to learn what to do with themselves when they didn't need to flee anymore. I found the Tamils were so used to handling a crisis situation, they had little experience in trying to manage life without danger and the reactive fight or flight response to survival.

The boat journey from Sri Lanka takes an average of twenty-four days, there is never enough food or water and people arrive in a weakened state, dehydrated and traumatised. It was not unusual to hear of deaths on the boat forcing other passengers to throw the bodies overboard. I met quite a few passengers of a boat of fifty men, women and children who had not only run out of fuel on their journey but had travelled through a cyclone, they were drifting at sea when a passing ship on its way to Sri Lanka found them. Some of the ship crew were Tamil and gave them fuel, food and water before they went on their way, but not long after the ship left the small boat was swamped with water and they lost the GPS. After five more days drifting at sea, five young men attempted to swim for help when they saw a passing vessel. The others on board begged them not to take the risk but the young men, distressed by the crying of the babies and children on board, were desperate to get help. They were aged between eighteen and twenty-two years old, all drowned, ironically their boat was found one day later with the remaining passengers rescued and taken to the Cocos Islands and then onto Christmas Island. When the survivors shared this story, they wept for the lost lives and opportunities the young men were denied, they each felt deep survivor guilt and I repeatedly heard from them how they wished they could go back to that moment to stop the young men diving into the water.

On occasion I met some Sri Lankans who survived not only the horrors of war but also the terror and devastation of the 2004 tsunami. Chajan is one of my ex-clients existing vividly in my memory because he had endured so much in his life and yet remarkably he remained grateful and talked about feeling blessed. His eyes were ink black, they somehow matched his sinewy fine form, skin leathered from years working under the sun. Dressed in the regulation tee-shirt and tracksuit pants it wasn't hard to imagine him wearing his Sri Lankan sarong.

Back in 2004 he had been living a simple life as a fisherman. He was married with five children and was content with life. The war progressed around him but it had been that way for so many years that he kept working and living as best he could and remained removed from politics. At nine in the morning on Sunday December twenty-sixth he left his wife and children to go to a friend's house up a hill to mend fishing nets. This was a common pastime for Chajan, his friends were all fishermen and they relied on each other to maintain each other's nets. They would talk about their children, about the price of fish, about the pressures the war impacted on them and about their dreams for their future, they assumed it was a standard Sunday morning but this day was one they would never forget. As they sat chatting they looked out to sea and witnessed an incredible sight, a tsunami swept inland engulfing Chajan's home and others beside it. It happened so fast and without warning they had only a few moments to jump up and run further up the hill where by chance the priest had suggested that the villagers celebrate mass for the final Sunday of the year instead of the usual church on the shoreline. Of the approximate nine-thousand villagers, three-thousand five-hundred were killed; among the dead were Chajan's wife, two sons and a daughter. He was left to raise his ten-year-old son Anthony and the youngest of his children, two year old daughter Kimaya who was found alive in a large floating cooking pot. How she landed into the pot and floated with her head above water is nothing short of miraculous. Chajan had an incredible smile on his face when he told this story, he said Kimaya had become a symbol of hope for many in the village and this helped him as he struggled through the grief of the loss of his wife and three children. He channelled his love into caring for his kids with the support of his sister and his mother who lived nearby, it was with them that he was eventually forced to leave his children while he left seeking asylum for them.

After the tsunami he was able to start fishing again with the help of foreign aid agencies from Germany. Fishing boats were provided to many survivors in an effort to return a livelihood to broken people. Unfortunately the Sri Lankan military had very different ideas, they gradually reduced the fishing zone to all Tamil fishermen in the region to the point they couldn't even take the boats out. The waters were heavily patrolled by the Navy and fishermen daring to enter out into the sea were shot at or imprisoned. With no livelihood and persistent episodes of worsening persecution Chajan was forced to flee, but he desperately missed Anthony and Kimaya and prayed their separation was going to be worth it. Chajan only lightly touched on the traumatic experiences in his life because he was completely focussed on his need to protect his loved ones, this strength and endurance was something repeatedly revealed to me and is what stays with me. I got to know Chajan over several weeks but there were many occasions I had a single meeting with an individual or a group that through the sadness of grief or unexpected laughter left a lasting impact.

The little Christmas Island Catholic church is a small building with a low ceiling it was in this sacred space we held a number of memorial services they were often solemn affairs designed to give space to grieve. When several Tamil men drowned on their way to Christmas Island I learnt of their lives through the survivors, I discovered they were a mix of Catholic and Hindu men so the volunteer nun Sister Dorothy arranged a small ceremony to honour both faiths. What started as a thoughtful gesture soon became a debacle when after everyone had taken a stick or two of incense to light at the altar the church filled with a dark plume of smoke, it hung just above our heads and gradually dropped lower and lower. The cheap incense Dorothy had bought from Meng Chongs the local Chinese grocers was used in the island temples but they were open air structures that allowed the incense smoke to escape, not so in the church. It was not long before our eyes were tingling and Bella started producing a dry cough indicating that her asthma was flaring up, I had to send her out of the church so she could breathe. Dorothy and I were looking at each with rising panic and with unspoken agreement sped through the prayers at a hilarious rate with our noses running and tears streaming down our faces, we unintentionally granted permission to genuinely cry for the loss of life. Before too long, everyone fled the building looking like we had bawled our eyes out for hours but in fact we found ourselves laughing together in vibrant solidarity.

It was while I was looking through my collection of memories from Christmas Island that I also came across another memorial flyer, which was printed on a double sided A4 paper in black and white ink. This time it was Sister Joan who had arranged the memorial service and once again I attended at the Catholic Church with the remaining survivors twelve months to the day. The flyer reads that on 1 November 2009, twelve Sri Lankan Tamils drowned in their attempt to sail across the Indian Ocean to seek asylum in Australia, their names were Jasmin, Veeramani, Kajan, Maapillai, Tharmenthira, Rajkumar, Mayuran, Mukunthan, Sinnathambi, Thileepan, Suresh and Rabash. The information describes the men being deceived by the smugglers into believing the boat they set sail on was temporary and that they were to be transferred to a larger and safer vessel while at sea; of course this failed to happen. After twenty-seven days afloat their vessel developed a leak and despite all their efforts they could not keep the boat afloat. Paheer was one of the survivors, he could speak English and was able to radio for help, nine hours later a fishing boat appeared, his testimony was included in the memorial 'we waved towards it, it came near us and we explained our situation then the boat captain said we have informed the Australian government and they have sent a ship'. Most of the men on the boat were unable to swim, Paheer emptied two oil canisters, tied them together and hung on in the big waves, they were 350 nautical miles from the Cocos (Keeling) Islands. After eight hours in the water they saw a ship. 'Around 6.30pm we saw a ship coming towards us, unfortunately before the ship came near us the boat sank, I saw that some of us were swimming towards the ship, others shouting here and there, in front of me I saw three people sink into the ocean'. Only one body was recovered the others were lost at sea, those who died included the boats captain and his young nephews brought to work as crew. One of the rescued was a nineteen-year-old who believed his father has been rescued, sadly he learnt that his father had drowned. Paheer said 'we never forget it, every day at night we see our people who are shouting *please help us* from the ocean'.

Afghanistan, Mustafa and Abdullah

My first exposure to Australian Immigration detention was back in 1999, I was nursing in Fitzroy Crossing in the remote Kimberley region of Western Australia. There had been a case of active Tuberculosis (TB) in the community and I was offered the opportunity to train with the Kimberley Public Health Service to deliver TB screening. I had just finished screening the Fitzroy Crossing community when I received a request to help with a large-scale TB screening of newly arrived asylum seekers. At the time the Port Hedland detention centre was full and several boat arrivals had forced the government of the day to open the old Curtin Air Force base outside Derby. I drove the 260 kilometres to help deliver the TB test known as Mantoux testing to hundreds of Iranian, Iraqis and Afghans over the period of two or three days, and then returned days later to do the follow-up skin test interpretation. I recall the camp as hot and dusty with very few trees for shade or greenery, the earth was red and sandy and people were housed in khaki military tents giving an impression this was only a temporary arrangement. There was a degree of urgency among the workers who were trying to accommodate men, women and children with limited resources, they were task driven and were not focussed on communicating with the new arrivals. I had never experienced prison officers or security guards before and I vividly recall being reprimanded for bringing in bags of lollies and balloons for the children, the rationale provided was that *they will just expect more*, the admonishment infuriated me and ensured that I brought more goodies the next day. My first impression of immigration detention was that it was necessary for the initial arrival stage to enable medical screening and to allow people to access to medical care. Curtin was very much a temporary camp and for the people seeking asylum they were all grateful for the attention and support. Unfortunately Curtin became a more permanent fixture with many families detained until it closed in 2002 following unrest and rioting. It was reopened during 2010 to accommodate adult men for extensive periods of time until it closed again in 2014.

Another of my past experiences was back in 1996 when I worked with Afghan asylum seekers and refugees for seven months in Mashhad in Iran. I was with the aid organisation Médecins Sans Frontières (MSF) on a mission to provide medical services to the largely unregistered asylum seekers. The Taliban, a radical political movement adhering to a fundamentalist version of Sunni Islam, had forced thousands of Afghans who practiced Shia Islam over the border into Iran. When I arrived, there were approximately ninety-thousand Afghans living in poverty in Gulshar, a shanty township on the outskirts of Mashhad and my job was to train Afghan health workers to deliver basic healthcare and importantly public health education to this ever-increasing population. This was challenging work. I would spend hours walking the narrow streets of Gulshar with the workers, as we visited house to house we would mark the top of each high metal gated entrance with a line of bright blue chalk to indicate we had visited, we had little to give but we were received with warmth and eagerness. The Afghan custom of honouring guests meant I drank enormous amounts of black tea and I sometimes copied Dara my interpreter, by putting a small block of sugar between my teeth and drinking the tea through it, sickeningly sweet when we needed a mid-afternoon lift to keep walking through the hot dusty streets during the summer or in the winter through the snow. I was delighted to spend time with the Afghans and Iranians once again during these few days in Curtin, where I practiced my woefully limited Farsi and Dari and attempted to chat about familiar places.

In 2008 there was a Taliban resurgence and they were once again targeting vulnerable groups such as the Hazara tribe. Forced to leave their country many people crossed into Iran where they faced more persecution and little to no chance of gaining the legal status required to stay permanently. The thousands of people who fled into Pakistan have been greeted with regular and indiscriminate killings; they have mainly relocated to Quetta a city near the border of Pakistan and Afghanistan now synonymous with acts of violence perpetrated against Afghan people. The Hazara are not the only victims in Afghanistan, however they are the main ethnic group forced to flee, with distinctive facial features highlighting their Mongolian heritage they become easy targets. Hazara are a Shia minority, while the Taliban practice Sunni Islam and will target anyone who does not conform to their ideology, for the Taliban it's easy to pick a Hazara in the crowd. The violence and danger faced in these countries of transit have forced people to flee further afield with Australia representing a place of sanctuary. One of the first Afghan asylum seekers I worked with on Christmas Island was Mustafa and his suffering became a very typical story.

When we met, Mustafa was about fifty years old he was married and the father of nine children aged between five and sixteen. He had been born and raised in Ghazni Province and was the son of a farmer and he had two brothers and two sisters. He told me that his mother had died in childbirth when he was young, which was something I would hear fairly often from an Afghan, the rate of maternal deaths in Afghanistan are one of the highest in the world. Mustafa was illiterate this was common among Afghans from the provinces who gained a limited education by attending small Islamic schools at local mosques where the Imam would teach the Quran and some ancient Persian poetry by rote. It was common for Afghan men to recite Hafiz or Ferdowsi and for the same men to be unable to read these great works. Mustafa had worked as a farmer, a street money exchange vendor and as a truck driver to provide for his family. In 1998 he was taken by the Taliban for the first time and they accused him of transporting goods for the foreign forces and demanded he hand over his truck, but he refused and was subsequently tortured and repeatedly beaten for days. He was finally released after he reluctantly agreed to give them his truck but the harassment didn't stop.

His brother was the next to be taken. He had been missing for two years when Mustafa told me his story and by then he assumed his brother to be dead. He explained how desperate he had become to find his brother and this desperation led him to approach a Pashto businessman who had strong links with the local Taliban, Mustafa met with the man to plead for his brother's life, but unfortunately this meeting aggravated the situation. The Taliban decided to target Mustafa's fifteen-year-old son Mohammad who was kidnapped and held for the ransom. Mustafa was forced to borrow most of the money and thankfully he secured his son's release, but the harassment and intimidation continued and he regularly received threats to his own life and that of his wife and children. The Taliban eventually returned for Mustafa and he was taken and locked in animal stables for six days where he was regularly beaten as they made demands for money that he simply did not have.

Mustafa could hear the sounds of military conflict around them so he took the opportunity to escape when his captors were forced to join the fighting; he fled to his sister's home where she dressed him in her burka and helped him escape to the city. Just three months later he was sitting opposite me in a stunned state. He told me how he had borrowed more money to pay a smuggler about three-thousand dollars in cash to arrange to get to Indonesia via Pakistan and Malaysia. He took a flight from Karachi to Kuala Lumpur where he was met by a group of men who led him to an immigration official they had presumably paid off. From Malaysia he took a boat to Indonesia, Mustafa said finding a smuggler to arrange a trip from Indonesia to Australia was not difficult, from there he boarded an overcrowded fishing boat with approximately one hundred others, they were all asylum seekers from Iran, Iraq, Pakistan and Afghanistan and he paid another three-thousand dollars. All this borrowed money would need to be promptly repaid and was a common stressor for asylum seekers arriving on Christmas Island. Many men were desperate to earn money to pay debts and feed families, this was not the only common link between them, Mustafa's boat trip to Indonesia was the first time he had been on a boat in his life and the sea was terrifyingly foreign to him. It was also the first time in his life to be separated from family. When we met he had not been able to make contact with his family and was not sure if they were alive. He told me *Afghanistan is like a graveyard now, full of all the people I love.* Unfortunately Mustafa's story was not uncommon and one that I heard many versions of over my years on Christmas Island.

There were also occasions when I met men like Abdullah, who was on his second attempt to enter Australia, it struck me that he was so used to running from danger that escape had become his identity. He was about twenty-four years old and had travelled from Quetta in Pakistan where he had left his wife, mother and sisters in a precarious situation. As the oldest surviving male of the family following the death of father and two brothers he carried immense responsibility for the survival of his family. He was born in the Kandahar Province of Afghanistan where his father had worked a small farm and in 1999 his older brother had escaped the Taliban uprising and was sent to try his luck in Australia but he has not been seen again. After the family lost another son to the Taliban in 2001 they decided to send their fourteen-year-old boy Abdullah. He arrived by boat on Christmas Island where he was detained for three months then transferred to Nauru where he spent a further fourteen months before being deported back to Afghanistan. Abdullah's father had died while he was away, so he returned as the sole provider for his family, he decided to sell the farm and head into Pakistan for safety. Unfortunately the security situation in Quetta is worsening all the time. During 2010 a single random terrorist event occurred targeting the Hazara population and by 2015 the events were happening each month, indiscriminate shootings in marketplaces, mosques and on public buses make life in Quetta dangerous and unpredictable. When I met Abdullah, he was desperately trying to gain access to Australia to eventually bring his family to a new and safer world, I truly hope he achieved this dream.

I have always found working with the Afghans humbling in many ways, they can be so polite and gracious, my colleagues and I would often observe it was rare to hear an Afghan complain. One dear Afghan friend strongly believes you cannot change the path completely just go along and accept the good and the bad. It is not a failed philosophy to live by, particularly when coming from such an unstable and unpredictable environment.

Chapter 2

One Day I Shall Have Freedom

Wherever men and women are persecuted because of their race, religion, or political views, that place must, at that moment, become the centre of the universe.

Elie Wiesel

Morteza

His emotions were almost completely blunted by the horrors he had been through over a three-year period. Each week as we sat in my office he displayed very little warmth or personality and I was often left wondering if I could be of any help to this man. The first time he experienced the brutality of the Iranian system was when his older brother was executed in 2003. The second time was when Morteza formed a friendship with a Christian man and he gradually over time decided to convert to Christianity. He told me that he had been seeking comfort and answers after his brother's death and that the forced version of Islam in Iran was not offering him any answers. Morteza began attending a Christian fellowship held in a private home; the group believed it was safe as they met in strict secrecy with all members very aware of the risk they were taking. After several months, members discovered the authorities had been monitoring the house after receiving information from a suspicious neighbour, eventually the group members were all rounded up and arrested.

Morteza was arrested at four o'clock in the morning he was blindfolded and taken to a prison where he was tortured and beaten regularly. He was missing for six months before his family were able to locate him, with his mother relentless in her search for him. He had a close bond with his mother and his eyes softened just enough to show there was emotion still buried in him when he mentioned her. As he described his treatment it was not hard to understand why this man was closed off from the world in many ways. He had been held for a total of three years in a small cell, taken out only for beatings and interrogations, when he heard a person approach the cell he was conditioned to stand, face the wall and cover his head with a sack. This psychological conditioning reduced his capacity to react in the world with routine emotion and would undoubtedly be a lifetime legacy.

Meanwhile, as Morteza was being regularly abused, his parents were petitioning the courts and took every opportunity they could to beg for justice. His mother sounded like a powerhouse of a woman, who managed to arrange for Morteza to be granted bail for one week with his parents' home offered as surety. Knowing that she was gifting the family home to the authorities, the family assisted his escape over the border. He fled to Jakarta where he spent four months waiting to travel to Australia. He did not get to see his wife and child before leaving Iran because they were deliberately left out of the planning to protect them, he also declined any opportunity to talk about them, it was too painful so our conversation simply didn't go there.

When Morteza finally climbed into the boat in Indonesia he thought the worst was over but when the boat capsized at sea, a six-year-old boy and a young woman were drowned. He was rescued after treading water for several hours and finally made it to Christmas Island on a second attempt. During a counselling session Morteza described the boat incident as *minor compared to the previous three years of hell in prison,* he was very convincing and I had no reason not to believe him. The suffering he had endured was immense and triggered horrific nightmares and flashbacks, I concentrated on managing these in an attempt to give the man some peace, but he was in a constant state of heightened fear ready to flee at any moment. Morteza had lost his belongings when the boat capsized, he arrived on Christmas Island with only the clothes he was wearing, he had lost everything, his wife, his son, his parents, his friends, his livelihood and his homeland, everything with the exception of traumatic memories of the past.

I worked with many Iranian clients and found one of the common reasons for an Iranian to flee their country is due to religious persecution. Iran is an Islamic state and although the government officially tolerates small groups of Christians, Jews and Baha'i, the secret police try to prevent any intermingling. In Iran denouncing Islam is a criminal offence that carries the death sentence, these sentences are perpetrated regularly by firing squad or hanging and convey that having your name added to an execution list brings certain death. It was not unusual for my clients to disclose they had escaped execution and for many of our clients to present as a direct result of persistent religious persecution and constant fear.

When I lived in Iran I made some great friends and was treated to the world-famous Persian hospitality. Justifiably proud of their culture there are not many Iranians who don't quote the great poets Hafez, Omar Khayyam and Rumi, but this national pride also hides darkness in the consciousness of Iranian people. I believe their psyche has collectively changed in their responses to each other, primarily in their ability to empathise and trust each other since the Islamic revolution of 1979. Since that time Iran has become a country that controls its people using fear and intimidation under the guise of government protective agencies, this has left a dramatic impression on its people.

The Army of the Guardians of the Islamic Revolution, otherwise known as The Revolutionary Guards or commonly referred to as Sepah is a branch of Iran's military founded after the Iranian revolution. The regular military defends Iran's borders and maintains internal order but the Revolutionary Guard was created to protect the country's Islamic system. Sepah has roughly 125,000 military personnel including ground, aerospace and naval forces and its naval forces are now the primary forces tasked with operational control of the Persian Gulf. It also controls the paramilitary Basij militia which has about 90,000 active personnel. The Basij are a paramilitary group of volunteers made up of ardent Islamists who willingly monitor, abduct, interrogate and torture innocent civilians and the level of fear and intimidation they inflict is astounding. There has not been a single Iranian I've counselled who has not been forced to flee due to persecution from either Sepah, Basij or in many cases both.

The time I spent living in Iran was an amazing experience and as it happened it was the first time I met with a survivor of torture. I was visiting colleagues in Tehran when I received an invitation to dinner at Dr Hussain Al-Shahristanis's home and to this day I consider him one of the most amazing people I have met. He is currently the Iraqi Minister of Higher Education but when we met he was lecturing at Tehran University. He is married to the incredibly dynamic Bernadine, an Irish woman who had spent years living in Bagdad making ends meet teaching English and raising their three children, while Hussain was imprisoned in the infamous Abu Ghraib prison. He studied chemical engineering in London and Canada in the 1960's and 70's specialising in the design and building of nuclear reactors, but it was in Canada that he met Bernadine and she settled in Iraq with him. He held high positions in universities and government agencies however when he was approached by Saddam Hussein to build nuclear weapons he steadfastly refused. His refusal led to eleven years of imprisonment, eight of which were in solitary confinement. I was hanging off every word when he shared his story. I remember sitting at their dinner table with Bernadine chatting with her strong lilting Irish accent and Hussain unpretentiously detailing some of his experience, such as pointing out the small holes in his earlobes as small markings of the torture he had endured. I was fascinated. Hussain had been repeatedly tortured over many years but he was determined that no matter what was done to him he would not build weapons for Saddam. He appeared an ordinary man however he was in fact extraordinary. He told me that Saddam had people so terrified they stood to attention when he phoned them and we talked about psychological conditioning and the impact on peoples psyche when they are exposed to fear and terror. I asked how he had managed to get out of the prison and he laughed and said Bernadine drove their car up to the prison in the middle of the battle during the first Gulf War. There was chaos throughout Bagdad and Hussain knew this was his opportunity because guards were abandoning their duties so he plotted a quick escape and he managed to get a message to Bernadine. She packed the children into the car and drove to the prison as Hussain found his way out, they drove over 200 kilometres through to the border into Iran, he laughed and said '*we are still driving that car*!' I was intrigued by his stoic personality and the dedication of his wife, they were so in love and devoted to each other. After his escape they added another beautiful little daughter to the family, born in Tehran she was their *freedom baby* and very much doted on. Hussain has returned to Iraq determined to be a part of the rebuilding of his nation and he was touted to be Prime Minister a few years ago, I wouldn't be surprised if one of his children leads the country in the future. Meeting Hussain gave me a small glimpse into the life of a survivor of torture but little did I know at that time that my future work would be consumed with these stories.

Living in Iran not only gifted me the opportunity to meet interesting people it also gave me the chance to develop a good understanding of the country and the level of oppression people are forced to endure. Just one month before I arrived to live and work in Mashhad, Sepah had raided the MSF office during a dinner party with consular staff from Kyrgyzstan,

Kazakhstan and Tajikistan. They took the local staff Dara, Hadi and Roya, blindfolded them, pushed them into separate cars and drove them around the city until they were completely disorientated, they were beaten and held in prison for ten to fifteen days. There were never any formal charges against them but the message was loud and clear, do not socialise with evil foreigners. As foreigners in a very religious pilgrimage city we were subject to almost constant surveillance, our phone was tapped, our mail opened and scrutinised, and our office and home watched. I also had two experiences that could easily have seen me arrested; the fear generated by these events was very real and enduring.

The first incident occurred during a mundane errand as my friend and interpreter Dara wanted to pick up his dry cleaning in downtown Mashhad. I agreed to come with him and when I saw that there was a big street procession on I told him that I would wait on the street and watch. The procession was an annual event in honour of the return from exile of the Ayatollah Khomeini and the beginning of the Iranian Islamic revolution; I had seen footage of these processions on the television back home and was intrigued to witness it in person. It was a very public and fervent display of anti-American sentiment, there were hundreds of students marching by me, with some stopping to burn the US flag. I was standing enthralled by the spectacle, watching everyone march by and then I did something ridiculously stupid, I reached for my camera. Within moments I was surrounded by at least ten plain-clothed police who corralled me into a vacant street corner, the police women aggressively patted me down while the police men were shouting at me, accusing me of being an *American spy.* I vividly recall becoming flustered and clumsy trying to find my identification in my handbag. My pathetically limited Farsi language skills where not helping the situation as I attempted to explain I was not an American but an Australian working for Médecins Sans Frontières. It's fair to say I was terrified when a small white minivan pulled up close to the curb and I was pushed towards it as the side door slid open. I will never forget seeing Dara turn that corner, there was a synchronised look of horror on his face and my own voice ringing in my ears as I shouted *Dara save me*. Dara did save me, he managed to convince them that I was not a spy or American or anything other than a foolish Australian. I can laugh about it now but I know it was a very close call, had they driven off with me in the van who knows where I would have ended up or what punishment they would have inflicted, I could very easily have simply disappeared.

The second event occurred a few months after my colleague Manana and I had met an American woman living in Mashhad; her name was Sarah and she had been married to an Iranian man she'd met at university in the United States. The marriage had failed but Sarah had custody of their three children on the condition that she didn't leave the country, she was surviving by teaching English. When we met she had started a new relationship however this had ended as soon as the new boyfriend found out that she was pregnant. She confided in Manana and me that she had arranged an illegal abortion but had not been able to go through with the procedure, she was trying to hide her pregnancy from everyone and wondering what to do. In Iran, women are stoned to death for adultery, there was little doubt that this would happen to Sarah because many people in her community opposed an American divorcee living among them and certainly would have made an example of her. Manana is a Georgian and knew of a couple in Azerbaijan who desperately wanted to adopt a baby and she organised a trip for Sarah. Manana planned to take her through the border to the couple where she would be cared for until she was ready to return after the delivery. We prepared to care for the kids and everything would be okay, or so we thought, until Sarah got cold feet and refused to communicate with us.

Manana went on leave and the phone rang at two in the morning, it was Maryam, Sarah's oldest daughter and the only one to know of her mother's pregnancy. She told me that her mum was in labour and asked me to come over and deliver the baby. The streets were covered in snow which as it happens worked in my favour as we usually had a Basij car parked across the road to watch and report on our movements. This was the one time they had something to report and they missed it. My first hurdle was getting to Sarah's apartment. We used taxis and they were always ordered by the interpreters Dara or Roya but I had heard them make the order enough times to order one myself in very limited Farsi. We had a list of taxi companies on the wall by the phone and I made sure that I used a company that we didn't use often to avoid a driver mentioning my late-night drive. When the car arrived I grabbed gloves, forceps and scissors from a surgical kit and I directed the driver through the snow-covered streets for twenty minutes. I arrived in time to run up a flight of stairs and deliver a healthy baby boy but I am not a midwife and decided that I needed to have a doctor check the placenta to avoid any postnatal complications.

Sarah kept repeating *I can't keep him, I can't keep him,* so I decided it was best if I brought her back to my house and office. I asked Maryam to phone a different taxi company and we bundled the baby up into cut up old sheets and blankets and I put the placenta into a plastic container. When I got to the office I phoned Hadi, a local doctor who worked for us and I asked him to come over immediately without offering any explanation, he arrived to find the new baby and mother in my bedroom.

Hadi confirmed the fewer people who knew the story the better, we decided to alert the authorities that a newborn had been abandoned on my doorstep which we thought would be plausible, due to the MSF signage. Hadi was worried that if the authorities were suspicious they would search the house, he advised that Sarah had to go before they arrived and before Dara and Roya turned up for work at eight am. There was only one main entrance into the property and we couldn't risk sending Sarah out there, in case she ran into someone. I searched everywhere and finally found a key to a small door off the kitchen that opened onto an alleyway. Just moments before Roya arrived, I pushed some money into Sarah's hand and sent her out the door into the snow, she was to find her own way home only three hours after she had delivered a healthy baby. The authorities arrived not long after, they took the baby without question but Hadi refused to make any enquires for me later as he didn't want to raise any suspicions. A few weeks later I told Sarah what she wanted to hear and what I wanted to be true; that a loving couple had adopted the baby and he was safe. Roya insisted on taking a photo of me standing in the office holding this precious little bundle, I still have that photo my face masking the immense turmoil of the moment. Had I not taken the baby from Sarah, I have no doubt she would have smothered her baby to prevent her own death and the removal of her other children. Sharing this story allows me to illustrate the level of secrecy and fear Iranians are forced to endure, it is an oppressive society and I believe it has changed the psyche of the average Iranian. It's well researched that living in a state of prolonged and heightened fear causes physiological changes to the body and I think it changes the spirit too.

Scientists have known for years that elevated cortisol levels interfere with learning and memory, lower immune function and bone density, increased weight gain, blood pressure, cholesterol and heart disease. Recent studies have also highlighted an increase in mental illness, notably depression. Cortisol is released in response to fear or stress by the adrenal glands as part of the fight-or-flight mechanism, the fight-or-flight mechanism is part of the general adaptation syndrome outlined by the Austrian-Canadian endocrinologist Hans Selye in 1936, Selye was known as the 'father of stress research'. He defined two types of stress, eustress (good stress) and distress (bad stress) both eustress and distress release cortisol as part of the general adaption syndrome.[6] Once the alarm to release cortisol has sounded the body becomes mobilised and ready for action, but there has to be a physical release for the cortisol to be released otherwise cortisol levels build up in the blood which wreaks havoc on your mind and body. For people like Iranians living under a fear-based regime the natural release of cortisol does not happen and this is where the change in psyche is evident. I see the Iranian situation as very different to people living in a war zone. When people protect themselves from shelling or bullets they also protect others, but if the threat is through words, allegations and intimidation then behaviours become closed off and secretive and people become less inclined to protect others around them, they simply can't trust each other. For days after delivering Sarah's baby I was restless and nervous, I confided in Hadi and he said *welcome to our world Chris.* He told me that every Iranian walked on eggshells and that they were all forced to hold secrets from each other and learn not to trust anyone but their closest relatives. This included people that worked for the Guardians of the Revolution, because people had a terrible habit of reporting on each other, even the most pious of clerics or soldiers had to watch what they said.

Reza

Now I am aware that I will offend some people with this breakdown of the new post-revolution Iranian but it seemed that when an Iranian arrived on Christmas Island they had used up all patience and tolerance trying to survive back home. They became known as the nationality that was intolerant, aggressive and sometimes bloody rude and there appeared to be a great sense of entitlement that was definitely not appreciated in the shared confines of the detention centre. There were frequent protests within the centre over the course of the five years I was there, some silent, some very vocal, symbolic graves were dug and lay in, lips sewn together, banners made, hunger strikes, self-harming and some violence, unfortunately there would often be Iranians heavily involved. The Iranians also became known for their racism toward Afghans and Kurds; they clearly believed the two groups were inferior, when I asked an Afghan man what was the hardest thing to tolerate in the detention centre, in a heartbeat he said, *the Iranians.* Having said that, I do want to acknowledge some amazing people who have been forced to seek asylum, my colleagues and I met some inspirational souls and heard incredible stories of bravery, love and sacrifice, Reza's story was one of them. The reason I connected with this story was that Reza reminded me of the run of the mill ordinary Aussie bloke, he could easily have been my brother Juz, the hardworking plumber who I adore. He was not notable politically but he was decent, honest and kind.

We were sitting in my little counselling office on the pretty blue and white floral armchair and matching couch, there were two large windows looking out onto the garden at the rear of the hospital. In the tropics the greenery is vibrant and fresh something I always found to be uplifting so for that reason I liked to give the clients the view. I usually sat in the corner between the two windows in the armchair and the client was seated directly opposite me on the couch with the interpreter beside on the far end of the couch. This way the client and I were focussed on each other and the interpreter was a convenient little addition in the background, but not really in the picture. The seating was important because it made the client the central feature, this was their therapy session and I always wanted this fact declared on entry to the room. I recall a physical shift in Reza's body when he started to talk about his brother, I watched as his shoulders collapsed, he slumped forward on the couch and his voice dropped in volume. These was not deliberate theatrics it was the body expressing emotional upheaval and exhaustion, a sign I grew to know well as a prelude to tragedy.

Reza's brother Mohammad had been a computer programmer who became a person of interest to the police and the Basij after they suspected him of anti-government activities. It was due to this interest he was taken from his workplace and imprisoned for six months without charge and eventually dumped, injured and bleeding, at his parents' home. The Basij gave him time to recover from the physical injuries but came to his home some weeks later where they killed him and torched the place. Reza leaned in closer to me and whispered *from that moment I started hating the Iranian fundamentalists*. Seeking retribution, Reza went to any authority that would listen with demands that someone be made accountable for the death of his brother but he was ridiculed by the police and his aggressive behaviour backfired. He was arrested and imprisoned for three years initialling in Tehran and then, as he described, *sent to exile in Bandar Abbas,* where he was subjected to torture and regular beatings in an attempt to make him confess to anarchy. After his release he tried to get on with his life, he resumed work and although he wanted retribution for Mohammad's death he accepted that he would not receive this and decided to stay silent.

As it eventually played out Reza was driven from his homeland and the people he loved by fundamentalists masquerading as virtuous theologians. He was forty-one years old and had been born and raised in Tehran, the sixth of seven children where his father worked as an administrator in a government office in the human resources department while his mother was a housewife. Once again there are parallels with my family, I am the second of seven children, from a close stable family and I can easily imagine any one of my three brothers seeking justice if one of us were targeted in this way. Reza described a loving family and a happy childhood but unlike his brother he hadn't been very academic and moved from secondary school into a technical school where he learnt some welding skills. After he left school her served his two years of compulsory military service and then worked as an industrial welder and fitter and turner, travelling throughout Iran. Life was good and he was thinking of marrying and starting a family of his own. He was not the least bit interested in politics and so easily stayed out of trouble with the authorities but then life changed dramatically. The experience following Mohammad's death and his own incarceration altered him as grief and trauma does but he thought that he had seen the end of the misery until politics got in his way.

In 2009 the Presidential election campaign was a turbulent time in Iran any person of interest with a past history of anti-government activity was rounded up and monitored by the Basij and Sepah, Reza was one of them. Out of the blue he was arrested on a false charge of harassing a woman, he was clearly furious when he recalled the moment of his arrest and the understanding that he was about to be exposed to hell again. The justice system in Iran is notoriously corrupt with crooked judges and bent police, when Reza was arrested he knew his fate was sealed. His shoulders abruptly rose up in defiance as he described being found guilty and being sentenced to fourteen months imprisonment. Exposing his kindness, he said that he felt sorry for the woman because he realised she must have been forced to give false evidence to convict him and that when he saw her for the first time in the court room she was very clearly terrified. During his incarceration he was severely tortured for forty-five days. He said *I counted the days to stay focused*, it was a way of being in control in a situation that would be considered by many to be completely out of his control. When I first met Reza, I noticed his arms and legs were covered in burn scars and old laceration marks and I understood he needed my recognition of his markings of pain, this unspoken acknowledgment allowed him to release some detail. He told me the regular interrogation and torture he endured included inflicting pain from burns, cuts, deliberately breaking his leg twice and rupturing his eardrum. Following his release from prison his family were horrified by what they saw and decided he should leave the country, when his application for a passport was rejected the family arranged a smuggler. His parents were continually being harassed by the Basij and Reza was in constant fear for their safety, his life had been ruined by false accusations and a disregard for justice. Ironically Reza had been a model citizen prior to the killing of his brother and he most probably would have lived life content with the regime, never one to challenge the State or Islam and yet he was brutalized. The fact that he was targeted by the authorities and that his treatment was deliberate and relentlessly maintained over many years was something Reza could not reconcile.

Reza's story of torment was a relatively common one, especially for us working in the torture and trauma counselling field however, it wasn't the memory of torture rather the consequence of the fleeing that we saw people battle with. Fleeing the torturers meant leaving parents, brothers, sisters, wives and children back home under constant threat, unfortunately survivors of torture are far too aware of the depraved capabilities of the tormentor. This makes the worry for loved ones interminable and is often a trigger for mental illness. When traumatised people are detained indefinitely with months rolling into years it is little wonder that tempers flare, resentment grows and more and more people become mentally unwell. I was concerned this was the set pathway for Reza and searched for a focus in his therapy to prevent anger and resentment dominating his future life, over the course of several weeks I concentrated my sessions on love. Each week I watched as he slowly allowed himself to acknowledge the love he always carried for his family as strength to draw on and not the weakness he had concluded.

Kurdish Iranian: Saman

Iran is home to approximately seven million Kurds spread across four provinces and whilst the Iranians and Kurds share many cultural, traditional, and linguistic similarities they disagree over two issues. First and foremost is the Kurdish inclination towards greater autonomy, while the second sticking point is that most Kurds are Sunnis, making them a sectarian as well as an ethnic minority.

The Kurdish people have been fighting for recognition of a separate state for many years and there have been several significant attempts made by the Kurdish Democratic Party of Iran (KDPI) to establish their own state. The most costly saw the loss of thirty thousand Kurds in 1979 just two months after the Iranian Islamic revolution. The KDPI's armed struggle officially ended in 1996 but another Kurdish armed organisation emerged in Iran by the early 2000s. The Party of Free Life of Kurdistan (PJAK) started in 2004 and is ongoing to this day, the group is considered a banned terrorist organisation by both Iran and the United States. The Iranian government remains strongly opposed to any suggestion of Kurdish separatism allowing relentless persecution to be inflicted on the Kurds, particularly on the vast majority practicing Sunni Islam.

A Kurd in Iran will often be treated as stateless with neither of the two common Kurdish languages Sorani and Feyli formally recognised in Iran. Being stateless essentially means that there is no evidence of a person's existence; no record of births, deaths and marriages, no rights to purchase land or have legal rights to identification and ownership. A Kurd is not granted access to public education and health care and will often find themselves the victim of arrest, interrogation and imprisonment. Executions are part and parcel of the regime's repression as is the persecution of Kurdish activists. According to Amnesty International the Iranian regime facilitated over five hundred Kurdish executions during 2012 the highest number in fifteen years.[7] There are also frequent hangings in Iran of dissidents of all ethnicities and religions, the majority of which are Kurds, many Kurds who have been arrested and executed over the years have been political prisoners detained on vague charges of 'enmity against God'. They are frequently denied access to a lawyer and are subjected to maltreatment in prisons prior to execution by hanging.

One of the first Kurds I counselled for over a year was Saman he was twenty-seven years old and the eldest of two children born in Ilam city on the border with Iraq. His father had worked hard as an electrical technician and a driver and Saman told me that his parents tried to protect him from the persecution and wanted to give him the opportunity for a good in life so they did everything they could to ensure he accessed an education and a happy childhood. Saman was halfway through his year eleven studies when his parents and sister were killed in a car accident and his whole world collapsed. He was forced to leave school as he had no family to care for him, both sets of grandparents were no longer alive, his mother had been an only child and his father had one sibling in Tehran but they had little contact. His father has been married previously and had a son to his first marriage, immediately after the funeral his half-brother appeared and demanded the family home. At the age of sixteen Saman lost his family, his home and he was forced to leave school all within a few days, he was compelled to start working as an unskilled labourer on construction sites.

Saman had always loved poetry and in an attempt to introduce some joy into his life he tried his hand at writing, he soon discovered that he was good at it. Unfortunately, this caused him more grief after some of his works were published in small newsletters and distributed among the Kurdish community, the authorities looked upon his writing as anti-government propaganda. At the time he was living in an area dominated by Persian Iranians when one of the neighbours, a Basij member, was burgled they immediately suspected Saman, he was arrested, detained and repeatedly beaten as they tried to force a confession from him, after a week of this treatment he was released. Saman was a religious boy so it was not unusual when he decided to go on a religious pilgrimage to Karbala in Iraq, he crossed the border illegally not giving it much thought because, like all his fellow Kurdish people he had no legal documentation to travel so crossing illegally was the only option. On his return the same Basij man accused him of going to Iraq to act as a spy and he was arrested once again however this time they tortured him and kept him incarcerated for weeks. When he was eventually freed he decided to move to Tehran to avoid further false accusations from the Basij and to blend into a large crowded city. Saman discovered life as an Iranian Kurd was always going to be a battle, he endured frequent harassment, intimidation and blatant persecution over the course of the next ten years. He worked at unskilled labour jobs with no work rights and no legal status and he saved for years until he could have enough to buy false documents and escape, at the age of twenty-six he finally fled Iran.

When Saman was detained on Christmas Island he started writing poetry again, I was able to encourage him to write as an integral component of his therapy. His words were powerful and allowed him a release of emotion without fear of retribution and he was delighted when I used his poems in local exhibitions and when one was published in a newsletter for a mainland torture and trauma counselling service. Saman was detained on Christmas Island for over two years because the system was choked by lengthy delays with the processing of asylum claims. He received a rejection of his Refugee Assessment Status (RSA) and was made to wait an additional agonising ten months for the results of an independent merit review. It was during this long wait that his mood plummeted, I started to increase the number of sessions each week to extend the level of support and to encourage him. There were some days when he declined to come in, which was very unusual for Saman who was adamant that accessing therapy was an important component of his new life. One day he was waiting in our waiting room while I saw another client ahead of him, he excused himself and went to the bathroom. The Serco guard wondered why he was taking so long and forced the door open to find Saman had cut his wrists, he was taken into the accident and emergency room where when I saw him he looked me in the eyes and apologised for disappointing me. I was so desperately sorry for him at that moment and excused myself to flee the room to cry. After I dried my tears I returned to hold his hand while he received several sutures to both arms. This was the only time we had an incident of deliberate self-harm at our service and showed the complete despair this young man had reached. To add to his distress the Department of Immigration denied him access to our counselling service for several weeks after this event as a consequence for self-harming. The rationale was that he should not be rewarded for bad behaviour.

When Saman was eventually granted a permanent humanitarian visa I went to the airport to see him off, he was so excited, dressed in his smartest clothes with a smile that would light up the sky, he was about to experience freedom for the first time in his life. I encouraged him to continue to write, I hope to see more of his poetry someday.

One day I shall have freedom

I remain in the cage like a bird; For now the flying is forgotten
There is no inner hope for happy songs anymore; There is no voice of love songs from me anymore
My world is shrunk to this cage; My freedom seized in this cage
My freedom is neither water nor grain; In the name of freedom I am imprisoned in the den
But know, that the day of freedom will come; I shall see again the freedom beyond the bars
The day of flying in the sky will come; That day you will hear my happy songs
In that day I will fly high in the sky of freedom; I will forget my days in jail
On that day I will shout the word of freedom; For captured birds to believe in freedom
And every single bird in a cage will follow my chant;
One day I shall have freedom; One day I shall have freedom!

Iranian Arab: Maryam

The Arab people of Iran have lived for thousands of years in South Western Iran, they form eight percent of Iran's population and are deeply rooted in this ancient land. The largest Arab community in Iran are the Ahwazi Arabs, residing mostly in the Khuzestan Province in southern Iran on the border with Iraq. This area is known as Ahwaz by the Arab community and the capital of Khuzestan is Ahvaz. According to Amnesty International the Ahwazi Arabs are facing discrimination by authorities concerning politics, employment and cultural rights. When they do have access to education the Arab students are required to learn in Persian language Farsi and are deprived from education in their own language, they are also not permitted to publish newspapers and magazines in Arabic.[8] Most Ahwazi Arabs have lived in Iran for generations and they happen to be on the richest soil in Iran with their province producing ninety percent of Iran's oil revenue, but this wealth has fuelled resentment and they are systematically being forced off their land as the Iranian government compulsorily claims it. The bulk of Iran's 137-billion-barrel oil reserves lay beneath the soil of Khuzestan and despite the annual income from export of the oil reaching one hundred million dollars the majority of native Arabs of the province live in utter poverty.[9]

I met a lot of Iranian Arabs the majority from Ahwaz but there are also some Arabs from further south in Bandar Abbas who are discriminated against both for their ethnicity and religion because they practice Sunni Islam. They are not allowed to build a Sunni mosque and must meet to pray in secret, the rate of imprisonment and execution is high among the Iranian Arabs and it is little wonder that so many people are seeking asylum elsewhere. Of course, not every Iranian Arab had the desire to leave the country, it is home, it's been home for generations and there is still hope among many that conditions will change for the better and people need to ready themselves with education and leadership. One of these thinkers was Maryam.

Maryam had presence that gave her a slight edge over everyone else, I suspect this is why she found herself in a position where she needed to seek asylum. A naturally beautiful women with large brown almond eyes and high cheek bones she was not unlike a young Sophia Loren. She was considered quite unusual for an Ahwazi Arab because she was well educated and she also managed to juggle a successful career and marriage. She had been working as a journalist writing for a newspaper on social problems in Iran but some of her articles have been considered controversial and had offended the authorities. When she started to receive threatening phone calls she chose to ignore them however, things escalated when her home was raided and searched by the police. Luckily for her she was not at home at the time of the raid but the police confiscated her computer hard drive and found sensitive research materials into religions other than Islam. This proved damning evidence against her and she was accused of *Mohareb*, a wager of war against God.

The most common penalty for Mohareb is death by execution and because Maryam is an Arab she knew that she would not receive a fair trial. Forced to live in hiding, her family arranged for her to travel out of the country on a false passport to Malaysia, Indonesia and on to Christmas Island. She told me that she couldn't believe it had happened to her and she was struggling to come to terms with the sudden change in her life because it had all happened swiftly and dramatically. I remember meeting Maryam for the first time, even in her state of wretchedness she remained impressive, Maryam possessed something special, she was someone people would want to follow, she was smart, wise and kind, all the good things that a country such as Iran needed. She was also desperately sad, she was missing her husband and her family and she was truly grief stricken, she felt cheated because she had to give up all she had known and loved for a news story. We talked about her life back home, her dreams had not changed as rapidly as her circumstance and she was confronted with a new reality that no longer included her family and profession. It was a severe grief reaction brought about by unfair circumstance that I addressed with her, we talked our way through several sessions but it became clear to me that Maryam was still fixed on how unfair her situation was. It was undeniably unfair, Maryam had been compelled to flee her homeland simply because she had a bible and information on the Baha'i faith in her possession and of course, she was an Arab. It was also unfair that Maryam was accused of heresy when she had never renounced her faith and was still a practicing Muslim. I struggled with clients like Maryam because they were often seeking answers that I could not supply, I also battled to accept that life could be so incredibly harsh for so many people, that innocence is robbed frequently and injustice is familiar.

Chapter 3

The Angel of Death

Sometimes even to live is an act of courage.

Seneca

Fatima

Fatima carried exhaustion as if it were a heavy layer of skin she couldn't shed. At thirty-years of age she had endured life in recent years with the survival of her family her only purpose. An Iraqi Kurd she was from a persecuted minority group in Iraq, and although the Iraqi Kurds are not stateless, they suffer discrimination due to their ethnicity. Born and raised in Baghdad, Fatima came from a close and loving family with three sisters and a brother, they had always experienced some level of ethnic tension but had managed to live happily. Fatima married, had three children and lived through the invasion, the fall of Saddam Hussein, the shelling's, the car bombs and the general mayhem of war. Her parents and sisters fled and were granted permanent humanitarian visas to settle in Australia, her brother was forced into Kermanshah Iran, but Fatima and her husband and kids stayed in Iraq. Unfortunately, their situation became even harder after her husband took a security job in the Green Zone. The Green Zone is the heavily guarded international zone in central Baghdad where the foreign forces and the new Iraqi government are based, it was originally built as the fortified headquarters of Saddam Hussein's Baath Party.

In Baghdad local militia groups were attempting to destabilise any hope of independent governance, they targeted anyone working within the Green Zone and Fatima's family became a target. One day while her young son was playing in the street he was kidnapped and a ransom was demanded to be paid within five days and a drop off point planned. Through the help of family and friends they raised the money and her son was returned in the middle of the night. They saw his return as a second chance and agreed they were not going to risk a life again, the family decided that it was no longer safe to stay, Fatima and the kids were the first to go, they fled to her brother in Iran. Without legal status they could not stay and knew their time would be limited before the authorities came to deport them. Their next plan was to try their luck getting to Australia to be reunited with Fatima's parents and sisters however, they had no way of gaining a visa. Paying the ransom had depleted their funds meaning that Fatima's husband had no choice but to continue working back in Baghdad until he could afford to join them later, so her brother offered to pay and escort Fatima and the children to Australia.

They travelled on false documents to Malaysia and Indonesia and then finally boarded a boat to Christmas Island. When they arrived on the island they were told of the new immigration *No Advantage* policy and the reintroduction of the Regional Processing Centres on Nauru and Manus Island in PNG. They were told they would never step foot on mainland Australia and that having family living there was of no value to them, the new policy meant they were to be given no advantage. The first distressing thing to happen to them was a forced separation from the moment they stepped off the boat. Fatima's brother was sent to be housed with the single adult males in the purpose built detention centre at North West Point, while Fatima and her kids were housed in the temporary overflow camp on the perimeter of centre, in a place called Aqua compound. The conditions in Aqua were very primitive, families used shared bathroom facilities that were always in demand, this meant that people had to queue night and day to use the toilet or shower. The rooms were small transportable buildings colloquially known as 'dongers', with very little room to move they were roughly the size and shape of shipping containers. There was communal eating, virtually no play equipment or toys and when the weather was dry it was hot and dusty, when it rained it was a muddy quagmire.

From the very moment they arrived Fatima and her children each experienced deterioration in their mental and emotional state, the children started bedwetting, something none of them had done for a few years. They were all experiencing heightened trauma symptoms, for Fatima the nightmares were so vivid and frightening that she became fearful of sleep. The intrusive memories for each of them were out of control, they couldn't regulate the memories and the flashbacks of horror because they were now terrified. Fatima was extremely frightened of being transferred to Nauru, she had heard horrendous stories of abuse happening there and was scared for her children's safety. She was also extremely fearful that she would be taken away from her brother, she was completely powerless and the conditions they were housed in added to her distress. To reinforce the suffering, immigration workers had promised family visits to see her brother, who they missed terribly but they had only been granted two short visits in the four months since arrival and these visits had been conducted under the threatening and watchful eyes of a guard, as a convicted criminal would be treated. After I had met Fatima for the first time, I arranged that the family would reunite once or twice a week for three hours at our service, I invented a referral for her brother and children and booked them all to attend the counselling sessions for the morning. I would set up the back veranda of the hospital with games and food for the family and then see Fatima or the kids for their sessions as they needed. There was no guard present to intrude on their space and as a consequence the children responded happily with the love from their uncle.

Things were not that rosy for their Mum, Nauru started to become Fatima's greatest fear and she was fixated on it. This was a woman who had lived in a war zone, she had experienced the kidnapping of her young son, she had been forced to separate from her husband, she had fled through three foreign countries, taken a treacherous boat journey for three days with her brother and small children, but her greatest fear was an Australian operated detention facility on Nauru. Fatima was assured by her Immigration case manager that the family would not be sent to Nauru without her brother but I made several requests on her behalf seeking assurance that immigration would not separate the family and if they were to be added to a transfer list that her brother be added with them. Both Fatima and I had been advised that immigration would not separate them and that the current separation was a temporary arrangement for the time they were on Christmas Island, the Department of Immigration reported that everything was being done to ensure the family would stay together. As I write this I wonder why I was shocked at the time to find that immigration had added Fatima and the children to a transfer list without considering her brother, devious callous things like this happened all the time. It was the persistent complete disregard for humanity and decency that I find unforgivable. If immigration had been successful in sending Fatima and the kids on that flight, she would still be over there, her children would probably be some of the many victims of sexual abuse and her brother would be sitting in Manus Island rotting with the hundreds other men currently ignored and abandoned.

Early one morning Fatima received the dreaded three am door knock nicknamed *the Angel of Death* so named because at approximately three in the morning on a random day of the week or fortnight the detention guards would knock on the doors of families picked for transfer to Nauru. They would shove a black plastic bag at them and order them to pack their belongings, they would be granted just ten minutes to be ready. This was supposedly intended to prevent distressing goodbyes and unrest in the compound but what it did was increase symptoms of trauma, people became terrified of the night. They took turns patrolling the compounds to allow their friends forewarning if any activity among the guards was starting so they were alert to it and the already vulnerable people became even more frightened.

Fatima told me that when *the Angel of Death* called on her and the kids, they were ordered onto a bus with other families and taken into the main detention centre. They were made to change their clothes and after being roughly patted down all their belongings were searched. Fatima was crying so loud that she started wailing uncontrollably, her kids started crying too with the distress of seeing their mother so upset. When the detention centre nurses could not console them, a psychologist was called to assist however, she also failed to contain the scene, mercifully they were eventually taken off the flight list and declared not fit to fly. Fatima told me that when she met with her immigration case manager days later, she asked her why she had nearly been separated permanently from her brother, she was told *there just must have been a bit of a mistake.*

It took a few more months but eventually after serious suicide attempts by both Fatima and her brother and a marked deterioration in the mental state of each of the children, they were all flown to mainland Australia. They were finally detained together and gained access to ongoing care and support from external trauma counsellors and more importantly received regular visits from her parents and siblings. They have all since been released into the community on Bridging visas, and are now waiting to be processed onto temporary protection visas however, Fatima's husband remains stranded in Baghdad. For Fatima and her three little children the traumatic memories of their detainment on Christmas Island cannot be erased, the *Angel of Death* is as vivid and injurious as the war zone they fled.

Sudan, Zareb

Working with so many nationalities I felt it was important to have a basic grasp of the politics of each country of origin, I made sure I that I followed international news online and tried to keep up with world politics. Sudan always represented feuding war lords, mass displacement, civil war and unrest and that hasn't changed, Sudanese politics still confuses me, but what I do know is that the north and south have been divided and governed separately since 2011. South Sudan separated and became an independent country and although far from a peaceful nation it happened that the asylum seekers arriving on Christmas Island had travelled from the north in what is now known as the Republic of Sudan. The country has become famous for human rights abuse, continued civil unrest and tribal and military conflicts. It is a country of nearly thirty million people, who have endured wars, droughts, floods and famines. One man I met gave permission to share his story.

Zareb was about thirty years old when we met, tall and muscular he was naturally athletic, he always smiled and was very gracious when I welcomed him with a cup of tea. A first impression would suggest that he was happy with not a worry in the world, the father of two children aged seven and four years old he had been born in a small village one of ten children to a poor farmer. His family become displaced due to the civil war and they fled to a UNHCR refugee camp in Darfur, a place they have called home for years.

In 2003 Zareb was arrested and tortured for assisting with an international investigation into a massacre that saw twenty-five thousand people killed, he told me that he felt he had a moral obligation to become involved in seeking justice for innocent civilians. The authorities heard that Zareb had given evidence, so he was detained, interrogated and tortured by the militia, since this time he has relived the experience with vivid traumatic memories. The fear of recapture has been very real and he received many threats that the authorities will return for him. After ten years of living in this heightened state of fear, he decided to join a group of other men to seek asylum and left his parents, siblings, wife and children in the camp with the intent to send for them later.

His first attempt to arrive by boat was disastrous as the boat capsized and his two cousins and three men from his tribe were drowned, he survived by clinging to a floating plastic drum and somehow made it to land. He managed a second attempt and arrived safely but when he arrived he received shocking news from home, the camp in Darfur had been deliberately targeted in shelling and his family had all fled. He was told that his father, brother and sister were killed and his mother, wife and children were missing. Even though Zareb had an expansive trauma history it was eight months before he was referred to our service for trauma counselling. His case was prioritised and I was able to see him straight away after receiving his referral from the visiting Red Cross Tracing team.

By the time I met Zareb he had managed to make contact with a friend back in Sudan who had located his wife and daughter in a hospital, but he was told his wife had been raped and one of her breasts had been cut off, his mother and son remained missing. At this time the situation in Darfur had deteriorated dramatically, all foreign aid organisations were withdrawn and Zareb was unable to maintain contact with his friend and had no way of knowing if his wife and daughter were safe. The Red Cross tracing team had referred his case to the Red Crescent team in Dufur however they were also denied access to the area due to the unstable security. It was incredibly challenging to provide counselling to Zareb because he was still living the trauma, he was completely powerless and was forced to wait for the conflict to subside before the search for his family could resume. In therapy I focussed on reducing his anxiety and allowing him moments of distraction away from the constant waiting and worrying. He responded very well to simple mindfulness practices and grounding exercises, literally smelling flowers and feeling the grass under his feet. We would talk about the future, about amazing possibilities and incredible impossibilities which may be interpreted as trivial, but for Zareb it was keeping him going. I often discovered that people with the greatest losses and horror experiences had the least to say, as the Roman philosopher Seneca said, *light griefs are loquacious but the great are dumb.* My work took me to places of sadness that words failed to capture and people did not attempt to express.

Three months into our counselling sessions Zareb shared a development, he was able to contact his wife, she was back in the refugee camp with their daughter and some other family members. The fighting had eased in the area and although the situation remained volatile she assured him they were okay. Sadly his mother and son were still missing however his family and friends believed that they may have been granted sanctuary in a remote village with other survivors. They were unable to travel to confirm this, so they did the only thing they could, they hoped and they prayed.

Zareb is a tenacious character, incredibly resilient and he gains his strength from a strong faith in God and by adhering to religious ritual. He completed sixty days of fasting and felt that it was through this intense prayer and sacrifice that good things were now happening, so he remained positive and optimistic in his mood and he coped with the pressures of detainment surprisingly well. He once told me that people were protesting in the detention centre about being detained for so long *I don't know why they complain, I have never been so safe in my life!* I guess it's all very relative to life experience. When I saw him last he still didn't know if his mother and son were alive, but he smiled and asked after my own family with genuine interest.

Iraq, Ruhi

In March 2003 the United States led invasion overturned Saddam Hussein's government and in so doing marked the start of years of violent conflict with different groups competing for power. We can all probably recall the very famous image of the giant statue of Saddam Hussein being toppled, since that day there have been ethnic and religious groups fighting for power and the sectarian violence seems relentless. In December 2005, Iraqis voted for the first full-term government and parliament since the US-led invasion and although the country seemed to be quieting, the reality is that Iraq has enjoyed only brief periods of respite. Iraqis have had to seek asylum at different times throughout the past decade dependent on their ethnicity, religious practices, affiliation with foreign forces and political ties. The Iraqi clients that I have worked with have come from varied backgrounds; poor farmers, middle class business owners, ex-police, people who had worked with the US and allied forces, Iraqi Kurds and Sabian Mandaeans.

Sabian Mandaeans are a minority non-Muslim religious community who follow the teachings of John the Baptist and have lived in Iraq for over 2000 years. They have experienced many years of persecution due to their faith, however they were protected under the Saddam Hussein regime due to the fact they are master gold and silversmiths. Saddam was reported to call them his gold makers. Since 2003 radical Muslim clerics have delivered fatwas condemning Sabian Mandaeans, consequently they have been faced with a constant pressure to convert, leave, or die and many Sabian Mandaeans have chosen to leave. Their small community is being forced to scatter throughout the world putting their ancient language, culture and religion at threat of extinction. As it happens, Sydney now has one of the largest Sabian Mandaean communities outside Iraq, second to Sweden.

Forty-five-year-old Ruhi was one of the first Sabian Mandaeans I met and I must admit I had to do some research on the religion before I met with him. He was a married father of five children and his story is a very sad one because it is filled with the loss and grief that unfortunately is far too common among this small community. He was born in a city near Basra into a large and loving family, he told me that his father had died of heart disease in 2001 and he was almost relieved by this because the disintegration of the family and community would have been too much for his father to bear. His family had always worked in the goldsmith industry and in fact were not permitted to own other businesses as they are considered unclean as non-Muslims. They had experienced severe religious persecution in recent years and this had destroyed the close loving bond of the community with the majority of people killed, imprisoned or forced to flee. For Ruhi by far the worst experience was witnessing the public execution of his mother and cousin in 2006 when the entire family was forced to watch their killing as punishment for their refusal to convert to Islam. After this horrendous event his family were delivered a court order to leave their home, this forced Ruhi take his wife and children to Jordan where they were living as refugees. The family were granted refugee status however they knew the chance of resettlement was miniscule, wanting to start a fresh life he decided to head to Australia to reunite with his three sisters living in Sydney. Ruhi was travelling alone when we met he had decided to leave his wife and children safely in Jordan and send for them later, he certainly didn't foresee the Australian government policy of no family reunification for people arriving by boat. Ruhi's extended family, once living side by side in Iraq are now displaced between Jordan, Sweden, the USA and Australia. The past decade has virtually destroyed over 2000 years of unique culture and identity for the Sabian Mandaeans and their suffering continues.

The Iraqi stories were many and varied, however they all carry the same theme, people were running from genuine persecution and their life in Iraq had become far too dangerous to stay. The choice was never an easy one to make because no matter how appalling life had become leaving home means never returning to people, tradition, culture and possessions that have held strong meaning. Once these are given up there is little chance of recreating life as it once was, I believe it's too huge a concept for the average Australian to consider because we are so protected and blessed. With my own experiences of living a long way from home, any yearning for home has been softened with the knowledge I can freely come back to the familiar sights and smells of the Wimmera Mallee in Victoria to find it unchanged, nurturing and safe.

Kuwait, Tasmeen and Maheer

In 1959 Kuwait passed a Nationality Law that defined nationals as persons who settled in the country before 1920 and maintained normal residence there until enactment of the law, as a consequence about one-third of the population was classified as Bedoon, meaning without nationality. The current number of Bedoon is estimated to be as high as one-hundred forty thousand with most Bedoon in Kuwait descendants of Bedouin tribes that roamed freely across national borders in the region. They led a traditionally nomadic lifestyle that did not factor a need for citizenship and proof of identification; as a result hundreds of thousands became stateless. Kuwait considers the Bedoon illegal immigrants of Iraqi ancestry, since Iraq invaded the country in 1990, the tensions between Kuwaiti nationals and Bedoon have escalated.[10] Bedoon once made up the bulk of the armed forces and the police force, people who served their country loyally however after 1991 the government of Kuwait started to dismiss the Bedoon from their jobs, barred their children from public and private schools and revoked their driving licences. The liberation of the country from Iraqi occupation in 1991 is what we call the Gulf War and it's when the government stepped up its efforts to strip the Bedoon of their rights. Children born to a Kuwaiti mother and non-Kuwaiti father do not get recognition as a Kuwaiti national because citizenship in Kuwait is passed on to children through their fathers, not their mothers.

Lack of legal status impacts all areas of life for Bedoon their identity, family life, residence, health, livelihood and of course they are denied a political voice. This leads to unstable employment in the formal sector only possible through 'favours', Bedoon are forced to seek livelihood in the underground economy. Their vulnerable status and lack of institutional protection renders them exploitable in what has been described as a new form of slavery. We saw a consistent number of stateless Bedoon from Kuwait arrive on Christmas Island and each person I met had been forced to endure a lifetime of discrimination and hardship and were worn down by fighting an unwinnable battle.

Tasmeen was one of the many, born the fourth child of six boys and four girls, both his parents are Bedoon and since the end of the Gulf War in 1991 they have really suffered. In 1999 when Tasmeen was eleven years old he was kidnapped and raped, his captors released him and he found his way back home to his family. His mother insisted on reporting the crime to the police and the perpetrators were brought to the police station but Tasmeen said that the police were not very interested. He felt ridiculed and the only form of justice offered was a monetary offer to be paid to the family by the abusers. Tasmeen and his family were pressured into accepting the payment due to poverty but he has been driven by fury and indignation ever since. Tasmeen had been imprisoned on multiple occasions as a young adult and repeatedly persecuted by the Kuwaiti population for not having legal status, this left him emotionally hardened. With no formal education and no work rights Tasmeen worked long hours as an unskilled labourer in poor conditions, he scraped and saved every cent for several years to take his chance at freedom. The first thing I recall about Tasmeen was his disposition, he presented with a real chip on his shoulder and a blatant disregard for authority, once he had shared a summary of his life it was very clear to see what was fuelling his attitude. He had every right to be indignant as his life to date had been a narrative of injustices, his break for freedom was now being thwarted by indefinite detainment and once again a complete lack of control however, he was an angry young man that I couldn't help but like. Tasmeen was one of many guys that I met for a brief part of their journey as he was transferred off the island to a mainland detention centre before I could do some meaningful therapeutic work with him. I can only assume he received some benefit from the sessions he attended but I will never know because with hundreds of clients coming through our doors there is little opportunity for feedback, I hope he is doing well, he deserved a good chance at life.

Maheer was another Kuwaiti Bedoon who arrived as a seventeen-year-old unaccompanied minor in 2011, his uncle had been compelled to arrange a false passport and travel for him when Maheer and his family became targets from a militia group. Maheer had been born in Kuwait where his father had served for thirty years in the Kuwaiti army but of course after the 1991 Gulf War the Kuwaiti government discharged all Bedoon from the armed forces and effectively made the family stateless. The family was expelled into Iraq where they were not able to gain a legal status, since then they have been forced to live as illegal immigrants in abject poverty. Maheer was one of the youngest children from eleven kids, his older sisters had received formal education while living in Kuwait and they home schooled him to prevent him from being illiterate. His face would light up when he spoke of his sisters, they had really pampered him wanting the best for their baby brother. Just three months before we met, Maheer along with his older brother and his father were kidnapped by a militia group. Maheer was present when his father and brother were shot and killed in front of him, his captors had decided they were a liability, that they needed just the one hostage. They demanded a ransom for Maheer's life and his uncle sold some goods and borrowed the money to have him released, he also arranged for him to leave the country because he remained a known target. Maheer was an incredibly brave boy whose head was still spinning from the dramatic change in his life within three short months. Luckily he arrived before the immigration policies denied the granting of humanitarian visas this meant his stay on Christmas Island was not extensive. He was referred for counselling because he was very obviously frightened and alone, there were no other Kuwaiti boys travelling as unaccompanied minors or in the family camp at that time and the isolation was difficult for him. Once again I have no way of knowing where he eventually settled and what supports he received, my motive for sharing is to provide some insight into the difficulties facing the Kuwaiti Bedoon because they are largely unknown.

Syria, Majid

The devastation of Syria started with anti-government demonstrations in March 2011 as part of the Arab Spring, peaceful protests quickly escalated after the government's violent crackdown and rebels began fighting back against the regime. By July army defectors had loosely organised the Free Syrian Army and many civilian Syrians took up arms to join the opposition. Divisions between secular and Islamist fighters and between ethnic groups continue to complicate the politics of the conflict. I am certainly not an expert on the issue but I know it to be a monumental catastrophe. It's now developed into full-blown civil war with a staggering 470,000 people killed at time of writing, more than half of whom are believed to be civilians, UNICEF reported that over 500 children had been killed by early February 2012. Additionally, over 600 detainees and political prisoners died under torture by the start of 2012. Bombings have destroyed crowded cities, horrific human rights violations are widespread and basic necessities like food and medical care are sparse. The U.N. estimates that over 7.2 million people are internally displaced while thousands of Syrians flee their country every day. The risks on the journey to the border can be as high as staying, families walk for miles through the night to avoid being shot at by snipers or being caught by soldiers who will kidnap young men to fight for the regime.

Every year of the conflict has seen an exponential growth in refugees, in 2012 there were 100,000 refugees, by April 2013 there were 800,000 that doubled to 1.6 million in less than four months. Syrians had overtaken Afghans as the largest refugee population under UNHCR's mandate, this is a reflection of the continuous conflict and violence in the country. In 2012 the Syrian Arab Republic did not even feature among the top thirty source countries of refugees[11] it's mind boggling isn't it? The latest UN figures show 5.4 million people have fled Syria since 2011. To address the crisis Jordan's Zaatari refugee camp was opened in July 2012, it has become famous for the aerial footage of a city of tents in the desert. It's a truly harsh environment that's either covered in snow or dust and it is now home to approximately eighty-thousand Syrians making it Jordan's fourth largest city. We didn't see many Syrians arrive on Christmas Island while I was there, firstly because the war started in very recent history and secondly because people fled over borders close by, intending to return home when things had settled, never dreaming that day might not come. But in 2014 I did get to meet Majid, a young man who had fled from his home in Daraa in southern Syria, near the Jordanian border.

Majid's family have been traditional farmers for generations and in recent years he and two brothers moved into the construction building supply business to supplement the farming. The problems for Majid started with his eldest brother Yousef who as a career army officer became a wanted man after defecting to the militia. His old colleagues in the Syrian Army were searching for him, when they came to the family home they found Majid at home, while the other members of the family including Yousef were out harvesting the fields they simply took Majid instead. He was taken to a prison and held for two weeks until whilst intense battles played out around him, the prison was bombed and he was suddenly released by the Free Army. We never discussed what happened to him in the prison, he didn't need to visit that memory when he had other more pressing things to focus on. The family knew the militia would return so Majid's uncle gave him money. Preparations were hastily made for him to be smuggled over the border into an old Palestinian refugee camp in Lebanon, he was hidden behind crates in a refrigerated vegetable truck. The truck driver was paid to make arrangements for him to stay in a room at a friend's place within the camp and he was forced to wait there for five months until he took possession of a fake Syrian passport.

Majid had only just arrived on island when I saw him and at that stage he had not been able to make contact with any family or friends since fleeing to Lebanon six months prior. He had heard that the Daraa district has been razed through heavy bombing and there was nothing much left of the area and the casualty rate was very high. On these occasions my trauma counselling skills were not always put to use, instead I would look at practical help, if I found myself in a foreign land, displaced from my people and language I would want someone to guide me. I put Majid in touch with the Red Cross tracing team in the hope his family and friends had made it to the safety of the Jordanian camps, along with thousands of other displaced people. When we sat together we would talk of the developments in Jordan and Syria and I made sure that we didn't focus on the negative news, we often talked of peaceful solutions and family reunification. Majid's spirit was not diminished, he had the greatest reason to live and to dream, that was the love of his family and the hope they would be together again soon. The last I heard the Red Cross tracing team were still searching every registered camp with no success, the numbers fleeing were overwhelming the system of registration, making it impossible for families to trace each other's whereabouts. As for Majid, I believe he was transferred to the mainland which means he would be in the community on a bridging visa waiting to receive a temporary protection visa. I have watched the media footage of the thousands of Syrians fleeing into Europe and wondered how many people are lost and how many families are left searching.

Rohingya, Azmi

The Rohingya are a Muslim ethnic minority with an estimated population of 1.3 million from Rakhine State in Western Burma (Myanmar). In 1982 the Burmese government left out mention of the Rohingya in new citizenship law and in so doing, they declared the Rohingya stateless. The Burmese government effectively declared the Rohingya to be illegal immigrants from neighbouring Bangladesh and have made it impossible for them to seek any help. The current and past military governments in Burma have subjected this community to forced labour, religious persecution, arbitrary land seizure, and the denial of documentation of birth and marriage. They have no access to travel documentation and are refused the right to passports or national identification cards; they are denied almost all fundamental rights. Over the last thirty years, hundreds of thousands of Rohingya have fled their homeland into neighbouring Bangladesh and Thailand where they are exploited and vulnerable in the margins of society.

In 2012 the Rohingya received some international attention in the wake of the Rakhine State riots. The riots were a series of conflicts primarily between ethnic Rakhine Buddhists and Rohingya Muslims, there were eighty-eight deaths reported and nearly three-thousand homes burned to the ground, it was described as an attempt at ethnic cleansing. Their desperate situation hit the headlines again in 2015 when nearly eight-thousand people were found to be floating ominously in rickety boats off the coasts of Thailand, Malaysia and Indonesia with dwindling supplies of food and water. The governments of Indonesia, Thailand, Malaysia and embarrassingly Australia, refused to assist and actively turned the boats back. The government of Bangladesh finally accepted them allowing entry into their infamously squalid refugee camps.

When I started writing this book there were 140,000 Rohingya living in displacement camps in areas along the Thai-Burmese border where the authorities would not allow them to leave forcing many Rohingya to live in the slums and refugee camps in neighbouring Bangladesh. However, those figures have changed dramatically after an attempt at ethnic cleaning on a grand scale in August 2017, over 647,000 people have fled to Bangladesh since 25th August 2017. Forced to walk for days through jungles and mountains those fleeing included pregnant women, the elderly, children, the sick and the dying, the suffering is incomprehensible.

The Rohingya were arriving in small numbers the entire five years I was working on Christmas Island. Back in 2010 I had to do some research before I saw my first Rohingyan client because I was completely ignorant of this ethnic minority, I had heard of the plight of the Burmese Karen people but the Rohingya were new to me. International media and human rights organisations have described the Rohingya as one of the most persecuted minorities in the world and yet until fairly recently few people even knew about them. We didn't really receive all that many referrals for the Rohingya asylum seekers given the numbers arriving and the length of time they were detained. It was easily explained when I met the first couple of clients for they are incredibly strong, courageous people, they have endured immense hardship and had never really found anyone interested in hearing their stories. The concept of counselling is alien to some cultures, talking about your problems and seeking help can be completely new and it certainly was to the Rohingya. These people have endured life as an existence to be tolerated, every Rohingya has faced the loss of loved ones, displacement and dispossession to the degree that these are anticipated events, with no time to grieve loss or expect better fortune.

Back in 2012 I met with sixteen-year-old Azmi, he was travelling as an unaccompanied minor after fleeing from the Rakhine riots. He told me that the village he lived in all his life was constantly targeted by the Burmese military and that he witnessed the military stand back and do nothing to prevent the Rakhine Buddhists from burning their homes to the ground. He said that his family had been torn apart, his father had left to work in Malaysia to support the family but the situation at home had got worse after he left. Azmi's brother was one of the eighty-eight killed in the riots, this had forced Azmi to go further afield to help his family, he had never been offered access to education and was regularly being forced into unpaid labour for the military. I remember Azmi as a shy timid boy, he was very small in stature making him look younger than sixteen years on first impression and he deliberately did not make eye contact to be respectful. Azmi had already worked long days of hard labour since he was eight years old and this showed in his calloused young hands and hardened look around his eyes. I spent a long time explaining what it was that I did and what our service could offer but he remained guarded and suspicious. Azmi presented as so many unaccompanied minors, like the deer before the headlights, hypervigilant and seeking an escape route wherever he went. He was experiencing a response completely fitting someone born into a life of servitude and persecution, our sessions were focussed on Azmi's dream to experience freedom and to access education, I hope his dreams are coming true.

Somalia, Amal

There have been several young boys and girls who I have had the immense pleasure to meet in my time on Christmas Island, their lives were spared due to their personal bravery and the love of their families. These children had been forced to travel alone, over great distance and through several countries on their journey to freedom; they each witnessed horrors far too graphic for anyone to view, let alone a child. One strong, feisty and dynamic young woman is Amal, she has allowed me to share her story and it's an incredible one. I have no doubt that Amal is going on to a life of greatness, she was definitely sent to us in Australia as a gift and this is her story. To give the story some context it's worth knowing a little about Somalia, the land of her birth.

Somalia has become an increasingly violent and dangerous country to survive in for the past twenty-five years. Well documented as a country run by deranged warlords it has experienced a new government since 2012 however there seems to be an expectation that Islamist militant groups will attempt to depose the government and gain power. One such group is Al-Shabab, a paramilitary group of often drug crazed men and boys attempting to terrorise the country into submission. Al-Shabab advocates the Saudi-inspired Wahhabi version of Islam, while most Somalis are Sufis, it has imposed a strict version of Sharia Law in areas under its control, including stoning to death women accused of adultery and amputating the hands of thieves.[12]

Amal is beautiful, inside and out, with a broad smile she will often throw her head back with a loud laugh that never ceases to have a contagious effect. Born in what she calls *bushland* in a remote country area of Somalia she is the youngest of eight children born to her mother. Her father had three other wives and nine other children from them, some siblings died in infancy or as young children due to disease and poor healthcare. With three sisters in Somalia a brother who has been missing for several years and another sister living in Kenya Amal's is the standard gap filled Somali family. When she was five years old her paternal aunt took her to the city of Kismayo, a port city in the lower Juba Province to live with her and help in the household. This is a common practice in Somalia, when children are living in deprived conditions a relative will sometimes offer to take them in, but they will be expected to be a worker within the household, even as a five-year-old. And so at the age of five Amal became part of her paternal Aunts home, she learnt to cook and clean and although she had cousins her age and older she was not considered their equal.

Schooling in the area was not available so the Aunt paid for a tutor to come to the home to teach the children. Amal was excluded from this but the tutor could see that Amal was bright and very desperate to learn, she would secretly set tasks for her and gradually taught her to read and write. Amal described her life as very hard, she was expected to cook and clean and behave, there was no childhood as we would know. When she was about fourteen years old Amal asked her Aunt to allow her to study, by then she knew the value of education and was very keen to try access it. Her Aunt was adamant that she was to work in the household and that there was no need for her to be educated, they argued and Amal was told that if she wasn't happy she could go back to her mother in the country.

Amal had enough; she hated her life as a servant girl and decided to leave. She arranged to visit a friend of the family after she heard that the friend's mother was planning to travel to Ethiopia. The woman offered to take Amal however, after two days of travel when they reached the crowded border crossing the woman simply disappeared and Amal was forced to cross the border on her own. She watched other people board a bus and followed, she took a seat beside a Somali woman she came to know as Halima. Halima noticed that Amal was alone and she insisted that she come with her to her cousin's house in Addis Ababa. At the house Amal met Mona who offered her a place to stay provided she found employment, so Amal went to the market place and asked every merchant there if they needed a worker. She found a job selling compact disc's and worked long hours, mostly up to twelve hours a day. She was walking in the street from the market one day when she found an old book written in English laying in the dirt, she picked it up, looking it over she felt she had found something very special and she took it home to keep, the book was *The Alchemist* by Paulo Coelho. Unable to read the book Amal fantasised about its content and dreamed of the day when she could read it to discover its meaning; the battered old book became a treasured possession. When Amal shared this story I felt that the book found her, the message in *The Alchemist* is that fear is a bigger obstacle than the obstacle itself *'Tell your heart that the fear of suffering is worse than the suffering itself. And that no heart has ever suffered when it goes in search of its dreams, because every second of the search is a second's encounter with God and with eternity.'*[13]

Determined to read her treasured book Amal enrolled in English language classes in the evenings where she met a German woman who was shocked to hear of the poor wages Amal was paid. The women helped find another job working under improved conditions as a Nanny and housemaid for a woman from Zimbabwe. After a few months her new employer had to return to Zimbabwe and Amal found herself out of work, she finally contacted her family and was told that her Aunt had relocated to Kenya and that her mother had been very unwell. It had been over twelve months since she left and Amal decided that it was time to return to visit her mother in Somalia.

It didn't take long for fifteen-year-old Amal to regret her return to Somalia, the Al-Shabab militia came calling on the family because they had noticed the return of a young girl and they informed the family Amal was to be married to *an old religious man*. The family refused and they were given an ultimatum, hand her over or pay fifteen-thousand US dollars, money they did not have. Amal was forced to flee to family in Kenya and it was from there that some family members arranged her trip to Malaysia, Indonesia and on to Christmas Island. Amal once described her motivation she said she wanted to go out into the world and grab opportunities to work to support her family and she wanted to access education, *I was fighting for my dreams, no one else could help my family if I didn't do that.*

The journey to safety was a dangerous one, in Malaysia the smuggler locked Amal in a small windowless storage room for five days while he made arrangements to get her to Indonesia. She described this time as so frightening that she wished she was back in Somalia being targeted by Al-Shabab. From Malaysia she was sent onto Indonesia where the first attempt to board a boat in the dark night was dramatically altered when the Indonesian authorities discovered the desperate group of travellers. The smuggler told her to run, she ran into the jungle and hid until it was safe to come out, watching as a pregnant woman running with her was captured. Amal located the smuggler and he locked her inside a dirty old toilet for three hours until it was safe to attempt to board the boat again, this time the boat sailed and they journeyed toward Australia. The wooden fishing boat was old and started taking on water on the second day at sea, with the people on board bailing water until finally on the eighth day the boat sank. By then they were close to the top of Australia and rescued by the Australian navy, Amal said she couldn't swim and was accepting of the fact she was about to die when she was helped out of the water. The rescued passengers were taken to Darwin where they were accommodated in the Darwin immigration detention centre for a matter of hours then at 4.30am they were woken and ordered to grab their belonging and boarded a chartered plane to Christmas Island. Amal's only belongings were limited to a precious book wrapped tightly bound in layer upon layer of plastic, *The Alchemist* had travelled with her.

Amal was seventeen years old by the time she arrived on Christmas Island, traveling on her own as an unaccompanied minor on the same boat was another young Somali girl, the two girls became great friends I eventually got to know them both very well. Amal is a strong character, she has had enough of being told what to do and more importantly what not to do, by the time she arrived in the detention centre she was itching to access a formal education however what was offered was incredibly limited. She had already started English classes in Ethiopia so she eagerly picked up from where she had left off practising with the Serco security guards and her English skills improved out of sight.

Not long after her arrival onto the island Amal became medically unwell, she was flown to Darwin and admitted to the hospital for treatment, following her discharge from the hospital she was detained for a short time in the Darwin immigration detention centre, where she heard of a writer's group called Writing Through Fences. Amal joined the group and discovered the group had been created as an online writer's forum also accessible on Christmas Island, the writing group founder and mentor Janet Galbraith encouraged her to write poetry and she has not stopped. After her return to Christmas Island Amal kept a commentary in prose of her time in detainment. She wrote of the desperation and sadness of others around her, of the good and bad times, of friendships made, of the fear and sadness from the transfers to Nauru and forced separations. Amal was detained in the family detention camp known as 'Construction Camp' and referred to as 'CC', she started writing a weekly news report she named 'The CC Weekly'. In it she announced the weekly events within the camp, she interviewed both a refugee and an employee of the week and gave a running commentary of the activities on offer. Amal has a quick wit and cheeky sense of humour but this brought about the demise of the 'The CC Weekly' after she released an imaginary interview with the then Minister for

Immigration Scott Morrison on the Cambodian deal. It was frowned upon by the department of immigration, they it called *blatant propaganda* but I just happened to love it.

Amal's dream is to one day be both an investigative journalist and a human rights lawyer, she wants to be someone who informs and raises awareness of important events and causes and also bring about positive change. For someone so young she has the innate ability to get people to reflect and question and importantly she never uses her own exposure to tragedy and circumstance to elicit pity. Amal was detained as an unaccompanied minor on Christmas Island for thirteen months from there after repeated and prolonged pleading to the Department of Immigration and Border Protection by myself and the detention medical team she was transferred into community detention on the mainland. By the time she was settled on the mainland she had turned eighteen and was told that she was not eligible to attend school. In true Amal style she argued with the Department of Immigration officials until they relented and allowed her to be enrolled in a high school that delivers an education program aimed at young people with English as a second language. She was delighted to finally attend school for the first time in her life. It took over two hours to catch public transport to get there and then another two hours to get home but she has never wavered with her dream to access education. She is still working to achieve her high school certificate and to continue on her journey to greatness.

I WILL RISE
You now lock me in detention and damage my hopes, but it's like dust and one day I will rise.
You may avoid my sadness and send me to Manus, but one day I will rise.
You may hide the reality and break my heart, but one day I will rise.
Why can't you help me? I am a female of underage who needs assistance from you.

You may send me to other countries and shoot me with your words, but one day I will rise.
You may kill me with your hateful action, but it's like air, and one day I will rise.
I may have bad memories rooted from pain, but one day I will rise.
I may have left a fearful life full of horror, but one day I will rise.
I am an asylum seeker searching for freedom; I don't have anywhere else to go.
Does my mind upset you so full of thoughts?
Does it come as a surprise to you that whatever you have done to me I will forgive you?
Wherever you send me, as long as the sun rise and the moon comes up
I WILL RISE.

Chapter 4

Dehumanising

Do not neglect to show hospitality to strangers, for by this some have entertained angels without knowing it.

Hebrews 13.2

Jamila

In 1999 the first of a series of boats carrying people seeking asylum arrived on Christmas and Cocos Islands, to counteract this in 2001 the Howard government changed the legislation in the Migration Act. Christmas and Cocos Islands became excised territory for migration purposes for people arriving by boat, known as unauthorised arrivals. The powers were extended further in 2013 under the Gillard government to include arrival by boat on mainland Australia. This means an unauthorised arrival has no right to apply for a visa if they arrive in an excised area. Asylum seekers may apply for refugee status but there's no obligation to grant them a visa to settle permanently in Australia and they have no recourse to Australian courts.

The Howard government commissioned the building of the Christmas Island Immigration Detention Centre (IDC) in 2005. It was originally built to accommodate four-hundred people including families but it has only ever housed adult males. Built on the North West Point of the island a twenty-minute drive from the township it's simply referred to as North West Point (NWP). The place is essentially a large intimidating prison with one wing actually built with families in mind. I was stunned by this information when I had my first tour of the facility because it's so threatening. it left me wondering what sadistic bureaucrat would consider a place encased with heavy metal doors and gates, secure electrified fencing, constant surveillance and misery appropriate for children.

It was officially opened in December 2008 however, the Department of Immigration decided to use the old construction workers camp to accommodate the few asylum seekers that arrived in 2008 because it was less restrictive and more convenient to the township. It wasn't until 2009 that the NWP facility was put to use after Christmas Island received 2,726 arrivals by boat compared to 161 in 2008. At that time a decision was made to use NWP only for single adult males and to utilise the construction workers camp, known as Construction Camp (CC) for families and unaccompanied minors.

The Department of Immigration policy to provide access to torture and trauma counselling from an external stakeholder was derived from the recommendations following very public inquiries into two significant cases within the Australian Department of Immigration that when they became public knowledge in 2001 and 2005 caused outrage and debate across the nation. The first case was that of Vivian Alvarez Solon, an Australian who was unlawfully removed to the Philippines by the Department of Immigration and Multicultural and Indigenous Affairs (DIMIA) in July 2001. In May 2005 it became public knowledge that she had been deported, although DIMIA knew of its mistake in 2003 Solon's family had listed her as a missing person since July 2003 and until May 2005 did not know that she had been deported. When Ms Alvarez Solon came to the attention of the Department of Immigration she was incapable of explaining herself and defending her rights, this inability had tragic consequences not only for her, but for her children.

The second case was that of Cornelia Rau, a German citizen and Australian permanent resident who was unlawfully detained for a period of ten months in 2004 and 2005 as part of the mandatory detention policy. Cornelia was mentally ill when she disappeared from hospital and was initially detained at a Brisbane Women's Correctional Centre and later at Baxter Immigration Detention Centre. She was classified as a suspected illegal immigrant or non-citizen by the Department of Immigration when she refused to reveal her true identity. Her detention became the subject of a government inquiry which was later expanded to investigate over two-hundred other cases of suspected unlawful detention by DIMIA.

The botched handling of the two cases brought about the Palmer[14] and Comrie[15] Inquiries; they examined immigration detention management and general medical and mental health services. One of the many key findings was that the Department of Immigration had failed to recognise the needs of the mentally ill, a failure from which tragic mistakes were made.[16] The findings brought about the introduction of the Detention Health Advisory Group (DeHAG) in 2006.

The DeHAG was designed to provide the Department of Immigration with independent, expert advice on health policy, standards for health care services, data and reporting, and mental health training. Made up of key health and mental health professionals and consumer group organisations, the terms of reference outlined that the DeHAG would play a major role in providing expert opinion to the department. The DeHAG were to provide independent expert advice and monitoring of health care services for people in detention centres and related facilities, with a focus on the delivery of primary health care and mental health services to people in detention. Just twelve months after the DeHAG was formed two sub branches were created to focus specifically on infectious diseases and mental health.

In March 2013 the DeHAG was replaced with the Immigration Health Advisory Group (IHAG) with the rationale that the needs of health advisory had grown beyond the need for clinical expertise alone, but required a wider scope covering health policy and service within the detention environment. The terms of reference stated that *IHAG will provide the Department with independent expert advice to design, develop, implement and evaluate health and mental health care services and policies for people.*

How often the groups visited Christmas Island is a mystery to me, incredibly they didn't bother to come near us, we were providing a service that saw huge numbers of asylum seekers referred to us and consulted and yet our input into the needs of the clients was never sought. In their defence however, I made this observation very early on that whenever the Department of Immigration had visitors booked for a visit to the facilities they were tightly managed, the schedule was rigidly set, there was no allowance for casual conversation with any worker or asylum seeker to provide an unplanned meet and greet. God forbid, if the enormous inadequacies were to be discussed. When DeHag or IHAG visited the island, I would usually hear about the group's visit after the fact or if by chance I heard they were coming my request to meet was ignored. Our new team did meet with them in 2010 when the team leader at the time bullied his way into arranging a quick meet and greet, it was so brief and tightly monitored by the immigration officials escorting them that there was no chance we could engage in constructive dialogue and this was long before the cloak and dagger secrecy of 2013 and 2014. I can only surmise that the schedule was deliberately set to exclude our service as we were known to have plenty to say that would no doubt oppose the altered image the Department of Immigration wanted portrayed.

On one occasion in 2013 when I was leaving a meeting at NWP I literally bumped into the IHAG group being escorted into the building. I had met one of the members two years earlier and I grabbed this opportunity to ask him to contact me, I desperately wanted him to know what we had been witnessing and subjected to. I pushed my business card into his hand as he was being called away from me by a very anxious Immigration Health Liaison Officer. I can clearly recall the look of horror on her face when she saw me speaking to him, she couldn't get him away quick enough. When his group made their scheduled visit to the health service he broke away and made a beeline to our building. The group had been invited to conduct a planned visit to the health service where we worked, this tour unsurprisingly did not include a visit to us. While the other members of the group continued on with the tour, he joined my colleagues and me for a rapid-fire summary of the increasingly inhumane conditions within the detention centres that we were most concerned about. We also discussed the lack of regard for our clinical recommendations and the constant disrespect we were being afforded by the Department of Immigration. This unscheduled meeting was clandestine and spoke volumes of the level of secrecy and suppression our team were forced to endure. At this time our service was feeling under fire, we had experienced the insidious dismantling of our ability to have our recommendations acted on, our clinical knowledge and expertise was often being ignored and dismissed by public servants with no knowledge of healthcare and evidently no regard for the sanctity of humanity. Many Immigration workers failed to understand our constant reference to our duty of care to our clients, they viewed us as an inconvenience and considered that we were bleeding heart advocates, they clearly had little understanding of our clinical role and responsibilities. After meeting with the IHAG member, we were assured that our concerns would be added to the IHAG report, we felt momentarily respected and that we had been heard.

Not long after this, in December 2013 the Abbott government disbanded the group and offered the position of sole health advisor to the group's chairman and a former head of Joint Health Command in the Defence Force, Dr Paul Alexander. The official reason given was that '*The large membership of the group made it increasingly challenging to provide balanced, consistent and timely advice in a fast moving policy and operational environment, and therefore the decision was made to disband the group, and replace it with an independent health advisor*'.[17] The decision was widely denigrated, how one man, with very little mental health and trauma experience could offer balanced, considered and impartial advice on the health and wellbeing of thousands of asylum seekers is mysterious. Prime Minister Abbott came out the next day in response to the professional and public outcry and said that IHAG '*was a committee which was not very effectual*', I confidently suggest IHAG was not considered effectual in meeting the Abbott government agenda.

When the DeHAG was formed in 2006 the Forum of Australian Services for Survivors of Torture and Trauma (FASSTT) was consulted, resulting in a policy developed to address a shortfall in the management and care of asylum seekers with a history of exposure to torture and trauma. By 2009 it was clear that boat arrivals were increasing on Christmas Island, the Indian Ocean Territories Health Service (IOTHS) had tendered for the contract to provide the healthcare within the Christmas Island IDC, the tender was not successful. However they did receive a directive from the government, that IOTHS would provide the Torture and Trauma counselling service. The DeHAG recognised the need to provide specialist assessment and treatment by an independent T&T service and the logical independent service was IOTHS as it was the only other external stakeholder involved in health on the island. The health service is one of the many services in the external Australian territories administered by a government department. At this time it was the Attorney General's Department (AGD) they signed a Memorandum of Understanding (MOU) with the Department of Immigration and Citizenship (DIAC) creating the service. DIAC funded the positions for three Counsellor/Advocates and one Senior Counsellor/Team Leader and AGD employed us.

Throughout 2009 boats arrived carrying Tamils journeying directly from a war zone and at roughly the same time the Afghan government and international forces were having a hard time containing a resurgence of Taliban support, and more Afghans arrived. The capacity of the NWP IDC was initially increased from four-hundred to eight-hundred and then increased again to eighteen-hundred places and capacity was stretched.

By January 2010 our counselling service was fully functional and snowed under with referrals. Our team kept hearing from the clients that conditions were harsh; they were crowded and cramped, to add to this people brought their prejudices with them causing ethnic factions to develop within the compounds and tensions to rise.

Our funding arrangement came with a promise to supply consulting rooms in the rear of the health service however when we started we were directed to use temporary spaces. We were allocated a consulting room, the patient lounge, a storage/training room and used the community health room when we could. On many occasions we used the rear veranda because there wasn't a spare room available. I was the last team member to arrive and found the health service anything but inviting and there was resentment amongst the staff because they felt we had come in and taken their much needed space. We were adding to the already busy flow of asylum seekers entering the health service and not only that, we were doing something considered strange, counselling torture and trauma survivors, it was too weird for some.

We used the *'temporary spaces'* for two years before we were finally provided with consulting rooms. We were given a reconditioned transportable building commonly referred to as a *donger*. Our donger had a roof that leaked like a sieve, something we discovered was not the greatest thing in a tropical climate with high rainfall, we would often race for buckets and towels when rain fell. On the day workers delivered our building it was plonked down onto a large section of the staff carpark causing more angst among the hospital staff, we certainly didn't make favourite employees of the month at that time. As it happens the IOTHS staff did finally warm to us, by the end of my five years I was truly grateful for the support and kindness of many of the staff, by then we had shared many laughs and challenges along the way.

Having our own leaky building was wonderful because it meant that we finally had our very own sanctuary and I begged, borrowed and may have dubiously acquired furnishings to make the place inviting. It had a small kitchenette where we could make tea and coffee for our clients and we put large potted plants out the front, artwork on the walls, soft couches and armchairs in each small office and it was very welcoming at last. It was very important to me that our office space was inviting for our clients, we had tropical garden behind us and would often take our clients outside to walk and talk in the garden or sit on picnic rugs on the lawn, it was mindfulness in action. By far the best purchase I made was a simple tea set I found at a local garage sale, this meant we could offer the clients tea from a porcelain teacup, of course we were offering much more than a mere drink, we offered dignity in a teacup.

When people seeking asylum arrived on Christmas Island they lost their identity from the moment they set foot on the jetty, each person was allocated a boat number and for the length of detainment were referred to by that number. The institutionalisation started immediately, people were told where to sleep and when, when and what to eat, and all food and drink was served in plastic or Styrofoam. When clients arrived at our service they were called by their name, invited to sit on a comfortable soft furnished couch and we offered tea or coffee in a porcelain cup. The little reactions we saw in people when they were treated as honoured guests in our rooms was an amazing reward.

My colleagues and I worked very hard to deliver a quality service but I really struggled with the mindless bureaucracy and over time I had to learn to speak a new type of language to communicate effectively with public servants. I learnt that speaking with emotion and displaying genuine care for the clients was pointless and lost us credibility. I had to discuss the clients as products and remove any emotional connection to allow our voice to be heard. This really was foreign to me because it was the first time in my career that I found myself working for an administration that was not health focussed, I had always reported to other healthcare providers not bureaucrats. Within our own little walls we were all ardent advocates for our clients, we all shed tears of frustration and heartache at times but we had to keep that emotion in house. Amongst the verbal dribble I had to listen to and speak at times, it was of great importance to us to maintain respect and dignity for each client and so it was rare for clients to fail to engage with us or decline follow-up. And sure it's fair to say that for some they just wanted to get out of the detention centre for a few hours and escape from the mundane detention environment, we recognised that and were happy to comply. NWP is a good twenty-minute drive away, for the people detained out there the drive was therapeutic itself.

Our service functioned well when we were highly organised. This meant we submitted our weekly appointment schedule to the Department of Immigration each Friday morning, stipulating session times, the language group of interpreters required and occasionally a request for the same interpreter for continuity of client care, although this was frowned upon by immigration. Immigration interpreter liaison staff would coordinate the bookings, interpreters and the request for service through to Serco to transport the clients. We did have to compete with other agencies such as the AFP for interpreters, so it was often a juggle to plan the week. We also had frequent 'no shows' when clients had a conflicting appointment and had not been notified of the appointment or they had been transferred off the island.

Another key component of our work was the ability to work with interpreters, it was essential to our service delivery and because our service was funded by the Department of Immigration we could access all the interpreters sent to the island. We soon discovered the value in good interpreting skills, although the interpreters were all supposedly certified by the National Accreditation Authority for Translators and Interpreters (NAATI), some were definitely better than others. We each had many occasions when the interpreter would take over the role of counsellor, they were very clearly giving their own advice and meaning well, but it really wasn't ideal for our therapeutic practice.

The ramifications to a client following a bad counselling session were not too dire, but if a client had a dodgy interpreter in an immigration or AFP interview they could potentially be sent home. There were countless occasions when clients complained of poor interpreting, often they were too polite to interject at the time, not wanting to create a problem for the interpreter, but these occasions had disastrous consequences. Some interpreters brought their prejudices with them, for example sometimes a Kurdish Iranian would be allocated a Persian Iranian interpreter and the interpreter would intimidate the client as badly in a session as they may back in Iran. The same can be said for Persian Iranians with Iranian Arabs, Sri Lankan Sinhalese with Sri Lankan Tamils, Iraqi's with Kuwaitis and Persian Iranians with Afghans. Another complexity when working with interpreters was that many had taken the asylum journey themselves, they had received permanent visas and settled in Australia but the return to Christmas Island often re-traumatised them. It wasn't unusual to finish a session with a client and follow-up with a debrief session with the interpreter who was battling vivid memories of their own journey. On some occasions the interpreter had lost empathy and would say o*h, he thinks he had it bad; my story was so much harder!*

When Serco brought the clients to appointments they would often bring everyone scheduled for a morning or afternoon appointment at the same time, people could potentially be waiting for up to three hours in a waiting room. We had our own separate waiting room and over time introduced activities for people to do such as jigsaw puzzles, cards, Backgammon and Connect Four. We started doing collaborative paintings where I would usually do a rough outline of a picture and encourage people to paint sections of it, we included Serco staff and interpreters in this and it was very entertaining at times.

The team functioned effectively by establishing good strong relationships with immigration workers in client case management and the interpreter liaison team. We also tried hard to increase and maintain dialogue with the IHMS mental health team, because they were the primary source of referrals. Of course there were difficulties in establishing and maintaining these connections, my colleagues and I were all employed on long twelve month contracts but the detention centre staff were all on short term fly-in fly-out contracts. We battled with constant staff changes. Initially immigration staff would come to do a three-month secondment, then it became six months while the IHMS team had varying contracts, we were always just getting to know someone and they would leave making consistent dialogue a challenge.

One of the key immigration relationships to establish and nurture was with the Health Liaison Officer (HLO). This was an immigration worker employed as the first point of call for any healthcare professional treating an asylum seeker to discuss recommendations and actions for treatment. The role was non-clinical and people filled this position for six months at a time with no health experience and enormous responsibility. Needless to say it was a tough gig, but made harder when given to people with limited knowledge and this was one of the many immigration roles granting people with little training extraordinary powers. The HLO position was like any sole position, it only functions if the worker does, some people brought their political aspirations along for the journey and others saw working away on a remote island as an opportunity to escape a marriage breakdown or other personal turmoil. There were also issues created with conflicting personalities, the relationship between our service and the HLO was dependent on these variables and of course it was an uneven power base, they had the muscle to take privileges and authority from us and over time they did just that.

Very early in my time on the island I clashed with the HLO, this was before I realised that speaking with emotion and passion was frowned upon and got us nowhere. As her parting gift on the day she was booked to fly off the island to another deployment, she contacted my boss the Health Service Manager and lodged a formal complaint that I was *advocating for the clients too hard.* As a direct consequence the Department of Immigration removed the word '*advocate*' from our position descriptions, my boss simply rolled his eyes and called her *a dickhead.* I have always been amused by her complaint because to me and the health service I worked for it meant I was doing my job exceedingly well. However, it also highlighted the crude reasoning of bureaucrats when they misinterpret medical advocacy for flagrant provocation.

Of course, I did have to nurture future relationships with HLO's because our work depended on open dialogue. For example, following an assessment the T&T team would provide recommendations and advice to the HLO when we felt it necessary, this may be to highlight a mental or physical health condition or any other significant issue of concern. We would also notify the HLO when we wanted to add a client for discussion at the Client Placement and Preventative Meeting (CPPM). Held weekly at both NWP and CC this meeting was our only opportunity to sit at the table with all key representatives from IHMS, the HLO, Serco Well Being, Life without Barriers and Immigration case management, where we would present our clinical recommendations for our most vulnerable of clients to highlight their needs. We also liaised directly with IHMS and requested medical and psychiatric reviews and had weekly feedback sessions talking about the treatment for shared clients.

Another task we took on daily was checking the Department of Immigrations Nominal Roll, this was a detailed spreadsheet of all the asylum seekers detained on the island it included the client name, age, gender, nationality, language, date of arrival, any family members present and the location where they are accommodated. It's a huge document that changed rapidly with a new version generated daily, we would receive an electronic copy each morning and found access to the Nominal Roll essential. I learnt the value in checking referrals against the roll early on when one morning I made my way to the waiting room to meet a new client. I could hear her well before I got into the room and when I walked in I found a very distressed young women, crying hysterically and pleading in Farsi. Her name was Neda, she was the mother of an eight-month-old baby boy and was travelling on her own as a sole parent. On that particular morning she had been called to the counter of her compound by the Serco officer and told that she was going for an appointment. With no warning her baby was taken from her arms, handed to another Serco officer as she was ordered onto a waiting minivan without explanation. When the interpreter finally explained what had happened I asked the Serco officer why he took her baby from her and he said very blankly that *the baby wasn't on the transport list.* It was very clear that he had no problem with his actions and he was very good at following orders but was not an evolved thinker. Of course, I made sure Neda was returned to her baby immediately and when I re-scheduled her in the future I always added the baby to the request, unfortunately situations such as these that were not uncommon. This particular example occurred very early in the establishment of our service and I learnt not to expect things to run smoothly but to make every effort to create a smoother pathway. I also learnt that just because *I* would never treat a person like that, didn't mean that others wouldn't. For many Serco officers a job on Christmas Island was lucrative; they didn't want to jeopardise it by getting into trouble for not following the requests for service and they didn't always use what I would consider common sense; they were happy to follow the orders without question, which is the complete opposite to how my own mind works. After this incident we checked the Nominal Roll against referrals received before we booked people in and to save any incidents that would further traumatise people we booked the children to come with the parent if they were sole parenting. Checking the Nominal Roll also meant that we picked up errors on the referral, for example, it wasn't unusual to find the wrong language group recorded, our checking allowed us to book the right interpreter. Importantly we were able to ensure the client was still on Christmas Island at the time of the booking and this was vital because once the schedule was submitted we were unable to make last minute changes. The process involved in getting a client transported to us took time, so of course pre-empting mistakes helped us avoid empty session time.

Another important check list we soon found invaluable was the daily transfer list. When the boats arrivals increased so too did the rate of transfers off the island. This list was another essential tool that not only let us know if our client was flying off that day, but also told us who to take off the waiting list. The transfers were always an issue because we had no way of knowing if each session was going to be the last and this obviously has an impact on the therapeutic value and the client-therapist relationship when each visit is a potential goodbye. Somehow we made it work and we provided good care and quality work. We created a forward referral system, consisting of people transferred off island before we had been given a chance to see them, we would scan through the transfer list and notify the HLO and IHMS at the transfer location of the T&T referral.

For clients with an open case we were able to engage with the T&T service in the state or territory the client was transferred to. We worked hard to develop and utilise effective referrals and requests for service within the Immigration network and counselling services on the mainland. It was really important to us that we could enable follow-up for our clients however this became a real issue with the HLO at the time. She was adamant that no people had been *lost in the system* but you didn't have to dig very deep to hear anecdotal evidence to the contrary from IHMS and T&T staff elsewhere.

As a government funded service we were required to provide a monthly report to the heads of Immigration Detention Health in Canberra. On the first Tuesday of the month we would start the day at eight o'clock with a teleconference to Canberra. I submitted a brief report on the previous month's work and any issues we had experienced that may affect service delivery and I also submitted a spreadsheet of the referrals received and the number of consultations. We used this forum to discuss any issues, but although problems were frequently raised, they were rarely if ever resolved. I liked the chair of the meeting because I felt he was sympathetic to our needs, the problem was he used the language of the public service and his agenda was purely to see that the contractual agreements were being met. I think that he had some understanding of how client-focussed we were, which made dialogue easier, however he was still there to ensure that the statistics were in. We would usually start the teleconference with a bit of banter as other people dialled in from other locations, he would call me Chrissy a name that only a few family members and old family friends call me but I never bothered to correct him because we had a mutual respect in each other, although no real trust. I was alerted when something had not pleased him because he would refer to me as *Christine* and usually deliver a short dry cough before speaking, I found this a handy warning. Clients' concerns were not always mentioned because for his purpose they weren't relevant. Delivering a T&T service update month after month is superficial when the content is numbers only, we could easily have been discussing how many tins of tuna we had ordered and received that month. Things were all going along fairly well until in December 2012 I received a directive from the Department of Immigration that had a huge impact on our service delivery. We were no longer privy to the Nominal Roll, the transfer lists and minutes from the CPPM's due to the Immigration Privacy Policy, I remember requesting a copy of the Privacy Policy that day and being told I couldn't have it due to the privacy restrictions. For obvious reasons it made our work very difficult because we no longer had the ability to check the referrals for mistakes or missing data and we booked clients in not knowing if they were on or off island. We didn't know where our clients were sent so we were unable to provide a follow-up referral, reference to the *privacy policy* was quoted constantly and our service was treated in a very punitive and irreverent manner. The lack of respect still upsets me and I experienced endless occasions when my frustration levels went through the roof. When once we had made quick calls on behalf of a client to clarify an issue or make a simple request, we were now repeatedly denied access to simple information. I clearly recall a colleague making a phone call to the HLO as her client had a nine-year-old child with a cardiac condition. The client was understandably anxious and wanted to know how much longer they had to wait before they would be flown off the island for treatment, not an unreasonable request, but she was denied the information due to the *privacy policy.* What we experienced was a systematic devaluing and disempowerment of our service and this directly correlated with the re-introduction of the Regional Processing Centres (RPCs), it was clear to us that we were making the Department of Immigration increasingly anxious. They couldn't get rid of us because they had a legal obligation under their own policy to provide a service to survivors of torture and trauma, but they didn't want to be bothered by the service.

During the same period of time the Department of Immigration cancelled our therapeutic group program. We had been conducting small therapeutic groups for different cohorts, mostly women and Unaccompanied Minors (UAMs) but I returned from leave in early 2014 to be told that *due to operational issues* we were no longer entitled to conduct group work. I was forced to petition Canberra for weeks until they reinstated the authority, I am still unsure why this happened because the Department of Immigration refused to offer an explanation. I do recognise that one of the main causes of angst with the department was the content we documented as treatment recommendations for client care. These were sent via the HLO to be included into the client's immigration file and they were also included in the meeting minutes when the client was discussed at the Client Placement and Preventative Meetings. Obviously having a paper trail makes any government department nervous, let alone a department that could be scrutinised in the future for maltreatment, I was acutely aware of this and intentionally sent a second copy of clinical recommendations to the clients IHMS file.

When a person has been tortured, exposed to a traumatic event or both they will often present with a decreased ability to cope within the detention environment, to put it bluntly, incarcerating someone will increase any symptoms of trauma. Understandably we were strongly opposed to long-term detainment and detainment where there was little or no hope of access to evidenced-based treatment. We put this in every recommendation made for our clients, for most of our recommendations we stated the following: [client's name] *has been identified as a highly vulnerable client. It is recommended that access to long term ongoing trauma focussed counselling be facilitated, with the ability for a clinician to clinician handover. This recommendation is made in accordance to evidence-based best practice guidelines, specific to the complex treatment requirements of torture and trauma survivors.*

This obviously became a huge issue with the Department of Immigration. How could they transfer traumatised people to Nauru or to Manus Island when we kept documenting that it was against our clinical recommendations? To the public servants within the Department of Immigration it appeared we were being obstructive. When the centres on Nauru and Manus Island were re-opened, we advised against sending specific clients stating that the location offered no access to required treatment and transfer would be detrimental to their mental health. I received a directive from Canberra during the monthly teleconference that we were no longer allowed to document a reference to a regional processing centre as it was in immigration policy to send everyone. It appeared to me the only dialogue immigration staff could relate to were directives, devoid of emotion and that is how they engaged with us. Eventually they viewed our service as an inconvenience to be managed just as Serco staff did with many of our traumatised clients so there are no winners in these scenarios for when two heads butt they both walk away sore.

Client Placement and Preventive Meetings (CPPMs)

It is well recognised that our childhoods shape our self-beliefs, some beliefs are more useful than others, I have always doubted myself because of my looks. I have been a fat girl all my life resulting in a belief I am not worthy, and that I present myself to the world as weak, undisciplined and therefore should be excluded from success. I can rationalise and reason my way out of this thinking however it is never very far below the surface. During primary school when kids in the playground started chanting *'Ten Ton Tessie'* I understood it was a cruel insult but I had to ask my Mum what it meant. In high school on my lunch break I walked across the edge of the oval while the boys played cricket and when Shane called *'roll the pitch love'* to the laughter of the others on the field I felt a physical pain, closely matching a punch in the guts. The memory still elicits a dull ache at the point of contact. I didn't stick up for myself, I wasn't confident enough to speak out to challenge the bullies and none of my friends bothered either, cementing the less worthy belief. Sometimes the self-doubt seeps in again with a momentary gut ache, I self-talk my way out of it but the more important the meeting, the more vital the outcome, the greater the ache and the harder it is to prove to myself that I should be sitting at the boardroom table with everyone else.

When I first started acting into the team leader role I often felt this insecurity attending the Client Placement and Preventive Meetings (CPPM's) but attendance was vital for our clients because it was the only opportunity to be physically present with the other stakeholders in the detention system. Each Tuesday afternoon a meeting was held in the boardroom of the administration building in NWP to discuss clients housed in NWP and in later years families in the Lilac and Aqua Compounds. On a Thursday morning we met at the Phosphate Hill site to discuss the families and UAM's detained in the CC. To be physically present carries more authority and engagement, it also gave us the opportunity to brainstorm ideas or raise additional queries, there was great value in attending, and it didn't take me long to realise hideous inadequacies in the power of a public servant. In 2012 The Department of Immigration outlined the guidelines for the meeting; *The Client Placement & Preventative Meetings (CPPM) allow for all stakeholders (Department of Immigration and Citizenship (DIAC), Serco, International Health and Medical Service (IHMS) and Indian Ocean Territories Health*

Service (IOTHS)) to identify vulnerable clients of concerns who require active, supportive intervention and engagement by all stakeholders. This will ensure that their health and welfare needs are being met in their current placement and to prevent further deterioration. CPPM relies on a multi-disciplinary approach whereby the experience and expertise of all stakeholders can be harnessed to support placement and management considerations.[18]

From a health focussed perspective, the purpose of the meeting was to discuss difficult cases and escalate recommended treatment plans. These plans generally included transfers into mainland detention facilities, hospitals or into community detention on the mainland where access to longer term supports and care could be facilitated. From a government department perspective, the meeting was about protecting the Department of Immigration from future scrutiny and accountability for the mistreatment of people in their care. These two very different motivations were destined to clash.

The meeting agenda was sent out to each invited agency, IHMS, Serco Welfare, Life without Barriers (later replaced with Maximus Solutions) and to our service. Each client was identified by SIEV (Suspected Illegal Entry Vessel) identification number, otherwise known as the boat number, for example ABC/012 followed by the name, age and location in the detention centre. At each meeting the client was referred to by his or her SIEV number by the immigration staff and Serco staff, what I found distressing over the course of time was IHMS staff also using the number system as identifiers, essentially dehumanising each client. This really concerned me because I saw the replacement of a person's name with a number as a direct indication of a loss of humanity. For our service the client's right to dignity was essential, we referred to the clients by their name and then the boat number to clarify if needed, this became one of many irritations to immigration staff because we would not conform. It didn't make sense to a public servant that the need to maintain client dignity was paramount to us, of course when I attended these meetings I was representing more than the clients, to immigration, I came to represent an ignorance of the system. I could hear the subtext in their dialogue with me, *can she just shut up about this client's needs; can she just stop insisting that a client be moved to the community; surely, she can see that we are very busy and so very, very important and, Oh God we don't need an advocate in the room!* Ah the irritation of the T&T team and the major irritation of Chris Cummins. I would drive back to the office or home depending on the time of day after these meetings and crank the music up to blast away the frustrations, something loud and ballsy to scream my lungs out to like Pat Benatar, The White Stripes or The Angels and on other drives I could sing along to The Cure, Nina Simone or M People allowing myself to smile about a win. On reflection it really infuriates me that everything was such a battle when what was at stake was human life and suffering.

It came to be almost accepted practice that a client was on the CPPM agenda for weeks before action was taken, this was irrespective of being in severe physical pain or experiencing an emerging psychotic state or being at a heightened risk of deterioration in his or her mental state. I wrote a huge number of clinical reports outlining the negative effect the detention environment was having on clients of all ages, they are lodged in the Immigration and the IHMS medical files of my clients and yet they were often overlooked and unheard. Our service limited the number of clinical recommendations we made because we were always acutely aware that an overwhelming number of recommendations would further diminish our professional credibility in the eyes of public servants. It was clients with the greatest needs or simple on island alternative solutions that we made our advice, even then we were forced to watch people deteriorate so badly they become psychotic or suicidal because of a deliberate preference to ignore and disregard clinical advice.

Jamila was one of my most frustrating cases I was forced to advocate for, all the way to the then Minister for Immigration, Scott Morrison. The situation was exasperating because Jamila simply should not have been treated as she was and certainly not for the length of time that she endured on Christmas Island. At the time Christmas Island was overcrowded, the overflow temporary facilities on the outer perimeter of NWP, named Aqua and Lilac were full to bursting with family groups. Jamila was referred to our service because she was exhibiting severe symptoms of complex trauma. What I discovered when I got to know her was that she was an amazing woman, a true freedom fighter who has sacrificed so much for the Kurdish people.

Her thick white hair, beautiful high cheek bones and stunning green eyes gave her a regal elegance, she seemed to generate warmth that permeated the walls of the little counselling room and I felt myself being instantly drawn into her presence. Born 75 years ago in a city in Iranian Kurdistan Jamila has experienced increased oppression over the course of many years from the Iranian government against the Kurdish population. She told me that she divorced from her husband many years ago after he agreed under extreme pressure to work for the Basij; she could not tolerate his decision so they have had no contact for many years, it was clear she carried his betrayal as a deep wound. Jamila had risked her life and the life of her children for the Kurdish people and it was with reluctance that she accepted the time had come for her to join her children in safety. Her six adult children are spread between Australia, Iraq, Norway and the Netherlands.

Her initial plan was to join her two sons living over the border in Kurdish Iraq but access to them was always denied by the Iranian officials. While her children attempted on many occasions to get their mother out of the country she was regularly harassed and deliberately targeted by internal security, experiencing frequent arrests and interrogations and eventually after many failed attempts at leaving through legal means she was forced to flee. When I asked Jamila what made her finally decide to flee after all the years of misery she said she was at a point when she was feeling incredibly hopeless and overwhelmed and was considering ending her own life when a neighbour stepped in. This kind man organised everything, the smuggler, the entire trip from Iran to her getting on the boat in Indonesia. It was her first trip outside Iran and she was terrified.

When Jamila arrived on Christmas Island she had lost all her belongings, she had only the clothes she stood in and she was oblivious to the Australian government *No Advantage* policy, denying family reunification and settlement in Australia for people who arrived by boat. She was told that she would be detained until her transfer to Nauru for the processing of her asylum claim, it was explained to her that she would not gain access to Australia because she had arrived during a time when all boat arrivals would be sent offshore. Jamila had no idea where or what Nauru was and she could not understand why the immigration staff repeatedly insisted that having family on the mainland was irrelevant because in her mind her family were very relevant.

On my first meeting with Jamila I was struck by her personal bravery and her dedication to her people as she had endured increased oppression over the course of many years from the Iranian government and remained resolute, even after losing her marriage and her children. Here was a person who had endured and sacrificed so much for the rights of her people, she held a strong sense of cultural identity and of justice. Jamila was an absolute joy to meet, I found her feisty and vibrant and so gracious, I felt we should have been applauding her, not inflicting more pain. Her story included a long history of torture, incarceration and of being beaten severely on so many occasions it was too numerous for her to recall. Her wrist had been deliberately broken five years earlier while under interrogation and medical treatment was withheld with the intention to permanently maim her, as a consequence she has very limited use of her favoured hand.

When Jamila presented to me, she had multiple medical conditions needing attention, she was diabetic and suffered with hypertension causing frequent dizzy spells and headaches. She also had bilateral cataracts and expressed legitimate fear that she would never see her daughters again due to her deteriorating eyesight. Jamila was frequently tripping over and on more than one occasion she presented with a swollen knee and bruising from a fall, over time the fear of falling limited her mobility and enhanced her fear of future injuries. As if her medical problems were not enough, she also had major social issues because she was the only Kurdish Sorani person in the camp; she spoke just the one language and was at a great disadvantage unable to communicate effectively with anyone. The limited use of her hand meant that she struggled to shower, dress, wash her clothes and attend to simple daily chores. When I asked how she managed she told me that a kind Arabic lady was helping her but they were unable to speak to each other and used simple gestures to communicate.

Jamila had been referred to our service to manage her symptoms of complex trauma because she was visibly distressed by frequent intrusive memories. She often screamed out loudly when a flashback occurred but she found that this made her a laughing stock around the camp so in an effort to avoid being mocked by others she started to chew her clothing to muffle the sound of her screams. Another coping mechanism she developed was to suddenly get up and walk when a traumatic memory started, however this odd behaviour was observed by others in the compound and they often ridiculed her, she was unstable on her feet and her coping strategies increased her falls risk. Over a very short period of time Jamila's level of distress increased and so too did the frequency of her nightmares, traumatic memories and flashbacks. The detention environment was acting as a constant reminder of the multiple times that she had been incarcerated and was a great impairment to her treatment, her cultural and linguistic isolation kept her frightened and lonely.

When I discussed Jamila on numerous occasions at the CPPMs, Immigration officials would give an automated response that she had arrived *illegally* and was to be subject to transfer as was everyone else. IHMS would say, *I can hear you Chris, can't you try fix some of her trauma symptoms and we will push for her to get her cataracts done.* The feedback from the Serco Welfare worker was that they would encourage her to learn English and attend craft classes! I found the dialogue exasperating, dismissing the severe vulnerabilities of a seventy-five-year-old grandmother was disgraceful and infuriating.

Jamila was seen by our service on just seven occasions, she was scheduled for more appointments however there were occasions when she was not brought to the sessions. The number of sessions may not have been high however she made a lasting impression on me, she presented with very clear symptoms of complex trauma and on each presentation, there had been an increase in intrusive memories. She was becoming terrified of being sent to Nauru and yet was reminded frequently by Immigration staff that Nauru would be her destination. Her symptoms were exacerbated by the detainment within the detention environment and further intensified by her social and cultural isolation, separation from her family, her physical disabilities and numerous chronic medical conditions. Jamila was truly suffering and yet never once complained.

After repeatedly presenting Jamila's case to immigration and making no progress I received a visit from Sister Dorothy one of the catholic nuns providing pastoral care in the centres. She told me that representatives from a government advisory committee had been on a brief visit to the island and were flying off that day. I knew the Thursday commercial flight was scheduled for 4.30pm and I raced to the airport to track them down, I had met one man on the committee two years earlier so I walked up, reintroduced myself and requested a brief chat. The Immigration officials chaperoning the committee looked very anxious as I insisted the man sit with me and listen. I begged him for assistance with Jamila's case and he assured me that he was meeting with the then Minister for Immigration Scott Morrison on the following Tuesday and he would raise Jamila's case. We swapped details and I hoped and prayed some good would come of it, I was offered vague assurances that he would do what he could, but I didn't hold out much hope.

When I saw Jamila next it occurred to me that her family had not laid eyes on their mother for years and that her grandchildren would have no idea what she looked like because there had been restricted communication between them. I asked Jamila to bring her daughter's phone number to the next session and we phoned her from my office, I got her email address and I did a photoshoot of Jamila looking radiantly at the camera, I was able to send these through to her daughter so the family would not be shocked by their aging mother and be prepared for the Jamila of 2014. Jamila had told me her favourite colour was green, so I brought in a green scarf and beads from home and gifted them to her, the photos showed her inner and outer beauty and she was delighted. Eventually after eight harsh months of detainment on Christmas Island, continued petitioning that she was not fit for transfer to Nauru and a hell of a lot of angst to have her transferred to a detention facility on the mainland Jamila, was flown off the island. I'm not saying I made the transfer happen, I know that IHMS were trying on medical grounds too and after repeated emails to the man from the visiting committee I eventually gave up trying to get any feedback from him. I am not sure if the minister ever heard about her case, but I like to think that he did and that my insistent advocacy paid off.

I advocated for many vulnerable people over the five years however Jamila came to represent the disparity between two sides of a detention centre fence. She was the same age as my own father Frank, my Dad is now retired, greatly admired and loved by his family and friends, he is offered homage by our community for his valued contribution to society. Whenever I saw Jamila I was also thinking of my Dad, it seemed to resonate with me that they shared the same year of birth and I felt the level of respect should be equal. I kept focussing on the inequalities presented in front of me and the evident lack of honour afforded to older people seeking safety, the incongruity deeply affected me.

There was no doubt attending the meetings was frustrating to say the least and I was often managing the niggling ache in my gut while sitting at the table. The CPPM was the only opportunity for our service to present a case to immigration and to petition on behalf of a client. The process required that we outline why the client had to be added to the agenda and was it a preventive issue or placement issue. For example, a preventative issue would often be when there had been a marked deterioration in someone's mental state and we would want to offer a treatment plan to prevent further decline. A placement issue would be either requesting a family be housed together in the centre on the island or recommending community detention on the mainland.

To me the main source of frustration was generated from the dialogue around the boardroom table, with two very differing agendas, ours was purely health and client-focussed unfortunately not everyone had the same idea. The problem was, we would suggest simple solutions for some issues; for example, families that had arrived together were sometimes separated into different compounds and this would obviously cause great distress, so our recommendation would be to reunite the family into the same facility which isn't rocket science. The inane discussion from immigration staff and Serco Welfare staff after this recommendation would be along the lines of, *is a move really necessary? You know I saw the family the other day and they were smiling and laughing at the time so I think that they are doing alright. The bed state is very tight and too difficult to consider at this time.* Immigration would pipe up; *so, they are doing okay then? Well if that's the case I think we can possibly look at taking them off the agenda and leave things as they are at the moment. Obviously, Chris if there is a problem in the future then they can be added again … next* and I was dismissed. These outcomes would end with a rendition of The Angels *Am I ever gonna see your face again* on the drive back to the office.

Although the agenda contained many clients that were not being seen by our service we were able to provide consultation and advice and we would often receive referrals during these meetings or make suggestions to assist with treatment planning. After three years of this working very effectively I was mortified when Immigration officials decided that our presence was no longer required for the entire meeting. We were directed to attend the meeting to discuss our clients only and to leave the building, of course this did not go down well with my team. I fought it through to Canberra, but lost the argument when they repeatedly claimed it was due to the bloody privacy policy. The fact that others sometimes added our clients for discussion without informing us didn't seem to matter or that we were a stakeholder in client care, fully funded by their department. When this exclusion first started I would discuss my clients first and then the room would go awkwardly silent waiting for me leave, I found it degrading to be treated this way because it was evidently a power play and I was to be *managed*. It didn't seem to matter that I was still being emailed a copy of the full agenda and the minutes of every client discussed.

There was a high element of frustration felt by both IHMS and the T&T staff because as mental health clinicians we often felt undermined and dismissed. We found that the opinion from Serco Welfare officers was often considered with a greater significance than that of qualified and highly experienced mental health professionals. The Serco Welfare officers were generally untrained workers who had worked as client guards and simply applied for a position change, they had no formal qualifications and little to no experience. To have professional clinical expertise undermined by the personal opinion of workers with no recognised expertise in mental health is not only objectionable, but also unacceptable when the outcome has a significant impact on vulnerable clients. It was obvious to me that when minutes of the meetings are scrutinised in the future the Department of Immigration will look like they actually tried to provide adequate care for the wellbeing of the clients. Mental health clinicians sitting at the same table would find that highly questionable.

Chapter 5

Incarceration

The accomplice to the crime of corruption is frequently our own indifference.

Bess Myerson

Detaining people takes enormous energy and resource and it has proven profitable for many businesses and individuals either through lucrative contracts or accelerated career paths. Serco is the company contracted by the government to provide the people management within the detention network across Australia and they turn a tidy profit. They employ the guards, known as client services officers to man the gates and the compounds and the transport and escort team (T&E), they provide a wellbeing section linking in with IHMS to support clients and they also provide the activities and access to resources. Serco report to the Department of Immigration each month and the Immigration director of contracts will go over all the figures to make sure they have met the contractual agreement, if this is not met the company receives a fine known as an 'abatement'. The process is intended to make Serco accountable but I found that they provided the minimum needs to the clients to get them over the line each month, to increase their earnings and prevent any abatements. Providing the minimum needs ensured a financial gain, Serco is a billion-dollar UK-based company and is purely profit driven. They started the company managing prisons, with many of their senior management team gaining experience in the justice system, unfortunately the justice system is in no way connected with social justice and this was very evident. The French novelist Honore de Balzac[19] wrote *behind every great fortune is a crime,* I resonated with this, feeling that although Serco has not yet been found to have committed a breach of legislation, their ethics are unlawful.

The Serco activities team were always stretched for resources, they provided English language classes at different levels and until the government reintroduced the regional processing centres they delivered a class on Australian culture to help people assimilate. This was axed as soon as they decided that people would no longer access Australian mainland. There were music programs, art and cooking, different sports like volleyball, basketball, cricket, soccer and a gym, this all sounds marvellous but it was extremely flawed. To meet the contractual agreement Serco only needed to show these things were available, the level of interaction and attendance didn't really factor therefore, one gym that could accommodate twenty men when there are one or two-thousand men detained didn't matter, because they were meeting the agreement. The other activity that looked good on paper was the *Island Tour,* this was when Serco would take a minivan of people out for a drive around the island. The problem was they only allowed one or two stops at designated places, a temple and a lookout over Flying Fish Cove. The stops were time limited and dependent on the weather while the rest of the tour was done seated in a vehicle being gawked at by locals and tourists as some kind of novelty. Unsurprisingly people didn't enjoy the tour; they would talk about feeling deflated by the experience so many people didn't bother going.

When I first arrived on the island the activities within the detention centres were provided by the Australian League of Immigration Volunteers (ALIV). The ALIV volunteers were a bunch of extremely enthusiastic young people, often university students doing a month or more voluntary work. They were coordinated by the founder of the league, Gary Taylor who as it turned out, lost the contract to continue in January 2011 after the Sydney Morning Herald published a speculative article connecting ALIV and scientology. The article claimed ex-volunteers had raised concerns Taylor was running the group with a heavy dose of *wanna be* scientology, however there didn't seem to be any evidence to support the claim. When Gary Taylor failed to meet a deadline to provide his financial records to the Office of Fair Trade NSW he lost the contract. The agreement between ALIV and Serco was reported to be worth approximately five-hundred thousand dollars annually, although Serco denied that ALIV was providing all the activities and claimed that they just supplemented them. The ALIV volunteers said they were hard pressed to find many Serco activity workers or programs running. For what it's worth I personally thought the ALIV volunteers were wonderful, they brought vibrancy and compassion into an otherwise dull and hardened environment. When the school holidays were on they would run programs the island kids could attend alongside the asylum seeker kids, it was a wonderful interaction and a win-win for all the kids and working parents like myself on the island. My daughter Bella absolutely loved the activities and would come home at the end of each day telling me about her new *best friends*. ALIV shipped over an inflatable jumping castle for the kids in the family camp, they conducted creative activities in art and crafts, cooking, sewing, music and importantly, taught classes in English, Australian culture and yoga. It was an immense loss to every single man, woman and child detained after they left because Serco didn't even contemplate filling their shoes.

Admittedly there were some great people employed by Serco who wanted to help and do their best but they were constrained by the profit-based motives of the company and I knew of some Serco workers buying clothing and extras for the children out of their own pockets. There was also a regular change in staffing over all areas and staff shortages were common, this meant activities that ran successfully for a time would be lost when the staff member with the skill set left. Serco staff worked long hours but they could be known to eat their young, it was very much a band of brothers. I saw people come into positions with very limited experience progress due to pure nepotism, the management team was a tight unit and were expected to protect one another or they were out.

An interesting fact that I discovered only recently, was that the unaccompanied minors would see the young Serco workers at work and feel protective of them. One young girl told me that she had been exposed to an awful lot of hardship and had seen many terrible things in her own country but she knew the young Serco staff were very inexperienced and often naive. She told me she had wanted to shelter them as much as possible, this girl was a sixteen-year-old UAM at the time, protecting young adults who were in positions of authority over her. For many Serco staff it was their first job or a big chance to earn a decent wage and have an adventure by going to Christmas Island, and what they were faced with was confronting and certainly not what they had signed up for. They were taught how to cut someone down when they found a client hanging and they were often the first responders when people self-harmed by cutting their necks, wrists and body. They sat with people when they cried and told them stories of the horrors they had fled and for many Serco staff the vicarious trauma was shocking.

The response to the staff trauma and other significant mental health problems was to employ a Serco staff psychologist in an Employee Assistance Program (EAP). Initially it was a visiting position but it was made clear early on that the island needed its own service. The EAP could be accessed by any Serco employee but there were expectations that Serco management would not only know who was accessing the service, but why. I was told they even wanted to know what was being said in the sessions and they had little or no regard for client confidentiality and privacy. Serco managed their staff in the same style they managed the clients, using an authoritarian approach that was more often than not, disrespectful and intimidating. The fact that a staff member was experiencing a mental health issue was often played down, or denied until that person became very unwell and he or she was forced to quit. Serco staff were fearful of talking to their own EAP service because they had a well-founded fear that management often got rid of any problems. Of course, the majority of Serco declined this offer of *support* and sought help either in the bottle or at the local health service, which provided an emergency response. That was where we would come in and conduct a crisis mental health assessment, offer our treatment recommendations to the GP and offer ongoing support and counselling.

Another key component of the Serco immigration contract was to provide the food, the kitchen churned out millions of meals and tried to provide a nutritional meal that could appeal to most palates. They could not possibly achieve this with so many different cultural groups, as much as the Tamils loved a hot curry with plenty of chilli, the Iranians hated it. The vast majority of people were very grateful for any food but, when they were detained for months leading into years they grew very tired of the same diet, the same flavours and would complain. Mothers worried for their kids because they wouldn't always eat the food and it was very common to find that kids were eating only the bread and jam offered, supplemented with sweets they could purchase with a point system from the canteen. The men would often talk about washing their food, they washed the rice off and re-cooked it in a microwave to get rid of the flavours used, or would just eat two-minute noodles and biscuits.

We had wild chilli bushes growing on the island which packed a punch and the Tamils loved to add them to their food if they could. In some compounds they started growing veggies and chilli bushes, then a new ruling came in that chillies were not allowed. However, on some occasions powdered chilli was handed out at meal times, this too became contraband but the problem was that this ruling was not consistently followed, some people could have chillies and some people couldn't and this was yet another minor issue that became a major frustration. Little irritants do have a way of growing into resentment when people are detained, the problem starts with the fact that asylum seekers are not criminals, yet they are treated no differently to the hardened criminals that many of the officers had managed in the past.

When the centre on Manus Island opened up we had clients ask us if there was a chance they may be eaten by the locals on Papua New Guinea (PNG) because there were rumours going around of cannibalism and people were genuine in their fear. The other common cause for distress was the fear of rape. They had heard horror stories of the infamous 'rascals' of PNG and were frightened that they were going to be sent to a primitive land where raping and pillaging was commonplace, as it happens they were right to be frightened.

By December 2010 there were 3,052 people in detention on Christmas Island, the centre was operating at more than three times the capacity it was built for, NWP was bursting at the seams and people were struggling to deal with the cramped conditions. The NWP facility was adapted to meet the growing accommodation needs and the first thing to go was a whole section of the education wing, converted into dormitory rooms, then the visitors section was converted because, well no one visited. The perimeter was bulldozed and made way for the infamous *'marquees'*, the Department of Immigration was loathe to use the word *'tent'* because it conjured up pictures of what they truly were, makeshift temporary shelters. These large tents are what we usually see at outdoor weddings and festivals, they were converted into dormitory living and surrounded by cyclone fencing. The facilities were stretched to the max, while activities for the men were very limited due to the volume of people detained and boredom became chronic.

In April 2010, the Department of Immigration announced they were suspending the processing of asylum claims from Sri Lankans for three months and Afghans for six months. The rationale given was the government needed time to gather up-to-date information on the situation in each country, something as it happens they did with woeful inefficiency. The only thing achieved by the freeze in processing was an enormous backlog and lengthy detainment.

At the time the process on arrival was that people made their claim for asylum, then went through a series of interviews with immigration and the Australian Federal Police (AFP) people smuggling team to have their Refugee Status Assessment (RSA) completed. It became almost commonplace for people to receive a rejection of their initial assessment, I don't really know the methodology behind the RSA I can hazard a guess that it was not based on any evidence-based practice, more likely the old *eeny, meeny, miny moe* method. Once people received a rejection they were offered the opportunity to appeal the decision through an Independent Merit Review (IMR) tribunal, obviously, by its name the tribunal was independent from the Department of Immigration and the overwhelming number of appeals were successful. However, there were few people conducting the reviews and with the number of people arriving and number of rejected RSAs increasing, people were made to wait months for their review and then months again for the decision. The next step was a security assessment conducted by the Australian Security Intelligence Organisation (ASIO), once again there was a wait to be called for interview and when the assessment was completed successfully a protection visa was granted. It was this constant waiting for decisions that saw people become increasingly frustrated. The mental state of most people is tested in the detention environment and to see others around start to fall apart created a ripple effect. The incidents of deliberate self-harm and attempted suicide skyrocketed, immigration, IHMS and Serco were not able to contain the sheer numbers of broken or breaking men so the place was imploding.

Rioting started on Friday 11 March 2011 and was not contained until 18 March. The men housed in the outer perimeter compounds simply pushed over the cyclone fencing and ran into the jungle, but not before the marquees were burnt to the ground. Some guys camped in the jungle for a few days, others headed to a remote beach nearby called West White Beach, and they were eventually brought back by the AFP. The fire was frightening for the men who did not want to take part in the protest and for the Serco workers caught in the middle of it and it had a huge impact on the island community, with many locals becoming vocal opponents of people seeking asylum. The fire brigade and the Saint John's ambulance on the island are manned by volunteer groups and the volunteers became exhausted by the call outs night after night and the frequent sounds of sirens heightened fear among the locals. I was tucking Bella into bed one night and was disturbed to find a garden hose gun under her pillow, the normally quiet little island felt under siege with the riots the topic of conversation amongst everyone including the kids at school resulting in Bella feeling the need to protect herself.

The rioting had started with a peaceful protest after some men received a letter stating that their security checks would not be undertaken until April due to the backlog of checks to be done. There were about nine-hundred men and women who had been accepted as refugees but they were waiting security clearances from ASIO, this was an increase from three-hundred and thirty refugees in October 2010 and the wait was excruciating for some. Although the media reported the rioting as a random event when a wild group of ungrateful asylum seekers had gone on the rampage overnight, anyone who had anything to do with the detention centre knew that the warning signs had been there for weeks, if not months. The cramped conditions the men were held in were unacceptable for extended periods of time and the time had extended and extended again for these men. I remember driving past a group of asylum seekers who had walked out over the fences of NWP to march into the township, carrying a banner saying *Freedom,* slowly being followed by a Serco security van, they were smiling and enjoying their taste of freedom, but not for long.

The rioting was all over the news on the mainland and I was receiving anxious messages from my family and friends worried that we may be in danger. A Hercules aircraft was flown onto the airstrip, the wingspan is so enormous that a plane of that size can't turn around on the Christmas Island runway, it was spooky seeing things like this invade the usually peaceful island. The Hercules was loaded with the AFP riot squad and all their vehicles and equipment, they remained on the island for months, initially staying on stretcher beds in the old indoor basketball courts that ironically had once housed the first boat arrivals of asylum seekers a few years earlier. These men were constant eye candy for us island women and we would joke that someone was going to accidentally drive off the road looking at them training because they never ran with a shirt on.

The aftermath of the riots was chaotic, with many men charged with assault and property damage. The charges were based on security footage and witness accounts given by staff on duty at the time, unfortunately staff on duty were justifiably frightened and in the confusion and chaos their accounts were not always found to be reliable. In August 2011 an Independent review of the incidents at the Christmas Island Immigration Detention Centre and Villawood was released. It identified that *in this environment, problems of health, including mental health, increased, and detainee anger and frustration rose, often producing violent reactions and self-harm. The growing number in detention on negative pathways, that is, those found not to be a refugee at either the primary or the review stage, exacerbated the situation.*[20] The review highlighted the poor conditions in which the men had been detained and the unreasonable length of detainment. As a consequence of the review and the overcrowding we saw an enormous amount of money spent on the chartering of aircraft on and off the island. The charter flights took hundreds of asylum seekers to mainland facilities hastily set up to accommodate the huge numbers. The clients independent review process was improved slightly with an increase in the number of reviewers appointed but the damage was well and truly done to many clients, they suffered needlessly due to poor policy and flawed practices.

Behnam

The impact of the riots on some clients was so severe I was certain we would have a death by suicide. Having a criminal charge meant that the processing of a refugee claim was put on hold until the outcome of a trial, a conviction could mean that a person would not pass the good character test required to be granted a humanitarian visa. The majority of charges were for damage to Commonwealth property, but for many of the men facing charges there was little or no evidence of their participation. The length of time waiting to have the charges heard was extensive and for one of my clients I became anxious that he would take his own life.

Behnam was a very polite and friendly twenty-six-year-old from Tehran, he came from a very happy home, good friends, great family and very mainstream Iranian life. He was not particularly academic so when the opportunity came along for an apprenticeship he grabbed it and he worked with a gas company as a technician for eight years. It was during this time he started a relationship with a girl whose father happened to work for Sepah, the Iranian secret police. In Iran young men are required to complete two years military service, so Behnam took leave from work and went off to another province for the training. While he was away the street protests and riots were happening in Tehran after the 2009 presidential election, of course he was interested in what had happened and was offered a compact disc with images of atrocities perpetrated by the government. Unfortunately, he copied the disc and was showing it to his girlfriend when her father overheard. His destiny was altered at that moment, a file was created by the girl's father accusing Behnam of anti-government activities and they had the evidence with the compact disc. It was only a matter of time before he would be taken into custody, Behnam and his family knew that he was in very real danger and they made the hard decision to smuggle him out of the country.

He had been on Christmas Island for thirteen months before he was referred to our service, his Refugee Status Assessment had been rejected and when I met him he had been through the process of an Independent Merit Review hearing four weeks earlier. He had been referred because he was struggling with the pressure of a charge against him for property damage during the March riots, his mental state had deteriorated and IHMS requested trauma counselling. Behnam told me that he was accused of damaging a computer but he denied the charges, now I know that people may consider me a pushover, a bleeding heart that only sees the good in everyone, I'm not. When I met Behnam I just knew he was telling the truth, it didn't fit his character and personality to be raging through a compound deliberately wrecking the place. He told me he had left a book in the Serco control room of the compound and in the chaos of the riot he took the opportunity to race in and retrieve it, it was sentimental to him because his parents had given it to him before he left and he didn't want to lose it. The room was abandoned because the riot was out of control and some of the asylum seekers had already broken into the room and ransacked it so the damage was already done when he raced in to grab his book and get out. He admitted that he should never have entered the room and that he was obviously aware that the area was out of bounds however he was adamant that he did not damage anything. He was mortified when he was told that he had been seen by a Serco guard breaking a computer and that he would be charged with criminal damage and need to wait for a court hearing.

The wait was unbearable and it was delayed repeatedly due to the AFP supposedly gathering the evidence and the magistrate needing to schedule the proceedings and the time to fly to the island. Behnam was appointed a Legal Aid solicitor who got to know him quite well over the months, this man confided in me after the case was finally heard that he would never take on an asylum seeker case again, he was appalled at the lack of justice and humanity in the whole process. I watched week after week as the young man seated in front of me became thinner and thinner with yellowing fingers from smoking cigarettes down to their stubs, he chain-smoked and paced, his eyes sank deeper into their sockets leaving a sallow looking scared young man staring blankly at me during most sessions. His hands started to shake so badly that he started sitting on them to avoid me noticing, but then his knee would start a restless tremble. Behnam felt completely powerless, the only way for him to make contact with his lawyer was to make a phone call from the compound but the phones were always in demand, and he would often line-up for an hour and find that the lawyer was unavailable. He was also confused by the whole process as the legal system was a new experience for him and he was bewildered by the ordeal. He became increasingly agitated when we talked about the charges but he always maintained his innocence and was very distressed by the accusations. His fingernails were being bitten down to the quick and bled, if he wasn't chewing a nail he was smoking a cigarette which was something that he had never done until he was detained.

Over a short period of time he became more and more dependent on his friend Ali who had arrived on the same boat as him, Ali was a great support and they shared the same dormitory. One day they both received word that their merit reviews were successful and they were being recognised as refugees. Ali was told that he was going to be sent to Melbourne where he could start his new life on a permanent visa, Behnam was told that his security check had been completed however the minister would not sign off on the visa until after the trial due to the character restrictions. Behnam took himself to the bathroom and cut his neck with a razor blade, thankfully this suicide attempt was unsuccessful, IHMS started him on an antidepressant however he found that all it did was sedate him. The medication did not help with all the negative thoughts whirling through his mind, so he refused the medication, he struggled to sleep and when he did sleep he woke in a sweat from graphic dreams. He took to pacing the front of the dormitory at night and having catnaps during the day and he told me he was frightened that he was going insane. I was seeing him only once or twice a week but IHMS saw him daily or twice daily, he became withdrawn and rarely left the dormitory area and his friend Ali became very anxious for him. Finally a court hearing was set for six weeks' time, but it was adjourned for the second time and the date went from October to February and then Ali was transferred to Melbourne.

It was as if Benham's only lifeline was cut, he had grown to rely heavily on Ali and now he felt so alone, I petitioned for him to be transferred to a Melbourne immigration detention facility but the feedback was not good. He was expected to be present in court in February in the Christmas Island court house, they would not do video feeds and he was to stay. When I saw him at the next session I was really alarmed at how he was presenting, he had lost hope. My greatest fear as a counsellor is when a person loses all hope, they have no reason to keep going, he had taken a razor to himself once before and I was sure that a second attempt would be successful. I petitioned again, I recall the conversation went along the lines of *if he is forced to stay, he will die, I have no doubt about this, he has to be near his friend to get through this.* They finally agreed, one of the concerns raised by immigration was the fact that he might refuse to get on the plane to return for the court hearing, when I offered to have Behnam sign a contract promising to return and it was accepted. He was flown to Melbourne and his mental state improved a little, when the time came to return for the hearing he politely boarded the plane as promised. On the day of the hearing I was present to support him in the little court house, the interpreter appointed was kindly trying to calm Behnam and explain the process, but his trembling hands were very noticeable. The Magistrate asked for the witness to step forward to give his account of the events and this was when Behnam discovered who it was that had made the witness statement against him.

He told me later that immigration officials had refused to tell him which guard had accused him of the damage, when he saw the man take the stand he was shocked. He had always joked and laughed with this man, he had known him as a friend and believed the man would have known him well enough over all the months prior to the riot to be confident it was not in his character to have done what he claimed to have seen. The magistrate heard the evidence, or lack of it, it became very clear when the man spoke that his recall of events was blurred and conflicting, the magistrate found Benham not guilty and the ordeal was over. He was returned to the Melbourne facility and when the minister signed off on his case he was granted his visa. He had been detained for 562 days. Eight years later Benham is still struggling with anxiety and he is now a seasoned smoker.

The rioting and unrest of 2010 was followed up by a senate enquiry and recommendations for future management of the detention facilities. One of the recommendations was that Serco establish an Emergency Response Team (ERT) to be the first responders when there was unrest within the detention centre and to prevent any escalation. ERT were also used within the compounds to beef up security, particularly when clients had been sent to the 'behavioural unit'. They were also used to escort people on and off the buses and up to their seats in the plane when they were being deported or transferred to Nauru or to Manus Island.

It was a pretty hard gig if you had any compassion for humanity, but very few of the ERT questioned what they were doing and it was definitely preferred this way by their management and the Department of Immigration. I got to know one of the guys very well and he told me when they were calling families up to transfer them to Nauru everyone was incredibly distressed and highly charged, the ERT were asked to search through everybody's belongings, something he found very awkward. Women would be forced to stand and watch as these big burly men went through their belongings, including their underwear and he said it was done in a threatening way to cause more distress. It was the behaviour of his colleagues that really upset him, they would often be laughing and making fun and weren't at all moved by the distress of the women and children around them. He said he felt compelled to remain neutral when he was working in that role because it would have been perceived as weak by his colleagues had he shown that he cared. Although he said the behaviour really disturbed him, I was disappointed that it was not enough for him to challenge the behaviour or resign.

It was very clear that the process used in the transfer of the clients was enforced to intimidate. The clients were taken in darkness, transferred into a compound in NWP and held there for up to ten hours. The long hours of waiting psychologically broke many people, they boarded the plane in a diminished state, escorted into a window seat one at a time. Parents separated from children, husbands from wives, each seated with an officer on the aisle seat to maintain the high level of fear and intimidation. When someone needed to use the toilet, they were escorted to the toilet and made to use it while the door remained open. Hearing these stories of maltreatment was disturbing and made harder to bear when I personally knew the people being ridiculed and the terrifying uncertainty these transfers inflicted.

Age determinations

Age determination is the term used when immigration staff choose the age of young people who arrive without official identification. The Department of Immigration put a team of public servants together to meet this task and I assumed there would be a scientific method used to determine a person's age but there isn't. Wrist and dental x-rays to check the density of the bones and teeth have been ruled out in recent years as unreliable because the findings are affected by the ethnicity and socio-economic background of each person. When young people reached Christmas Island an immigration official would conduct an interview with the aid of an interpreter and a worker from a support agency either Life without Barriers or Maximus to act as an independent observer. There will be a series of questions, along the lines of *so how old do you think you are? Can you prove it? What have you been doing back home?* As there is no proven scientific method for determining the age of a person seated in front of them, the determination is based on the opinion of the worker and the quality of the interpreting. It was very common for boys to be determined older than what they were and sometimes for young men to be accepted as under eighteen years of age. In countries like Afghanistan and Burma there is often no official record of birth and birthdays are not celebrated occasions, so people know they are old enough to work or drive or marry because their family will tell them, but a specific date of birth is of no value or importance. People will often know the year of their birth because families will align the birth with an auspicious religious occasion or significant event for example an Afghan may know he was born in 1989, the year the Russians left Afghanistan. When asylum seekers arrive without valid documentation, a date of birth is issued by the Department of Immigration, it is usually the same day, there are thousands of people in Australia with birthdates registered on December thirty-one of any given year.

Mohammad

When Mohammad arrived he was sixteen-years-old, he had travelled from Afghanistan where he had already experienced a hard life, he was from Kabul and had two older sisters and an older brother and his parents had both died when he was eight-years-old. His older siblings helped to raise him as best they could but they were living in poverty and Mohammad had no access to formal education and started working when he was ten years old. He began as an errand boy in the streets of Kabul and then progressed to work as a labourer on construction sites, but he was young and vulnerable and often physically abused. After he was badly beaten and sexually abused by the police his brother decided that he would try to get him out to have a chance at a better life, so his brother borrowed most of the money needed for Mohammad's trip and sent him on his way. He travelled alone, a sixteen-year-old boy, through Pakistan, Malaysia and Indonesia and he had never seen the ocean until he climbed into the wooden fishing boat in Indonesia.

Mohammad talked about his family a lot, he had a favourite niece Fatima, who was only two-years-old and he missed her terribly. He also worried for them all the time as they lived from hand-to-mouth and the streets of Kabul are not safe. I had been referred an eighteen-year-old man from NWP but it was a child that sat opposite me. He was very clearly sixteen or maybe younger, when I asked what the immigration worker had asked him he said *she asked me about myself, so I told her, I worked here for a year and there for a year and did this and did that. She looked at me and said then you must be over eighteen,* that was it, he was age determined.

For Mohammad, I didn't bother fighting it, he assured me he felt safe in the compound where he was housed with the other Afghans he was sharing a room with. He was street smart, but he was still a child being housed with the single adult males. It was a different story for another boy that I once added to the CPPM agenda, He was very frightened and distressed by being determined older than he was. The immigration staff told me that it was pointless they said *no one had their decisions reversed* because the new birthdate was on all documentation and they were reluctant to change it. Having the wrong year of birth on a child's documentation had very dangerous consequences because young boys were sent to Manus Island and when the Salvation Army and IHMS raised this as a concern for the safety and wellbeing for the boys, it was ignored by the Department of Immigration.

Personal safety was not the only problem created with the wrong age determination, children were also denied their opportunity for education and support, as limited as it was. The kids wrongly age determined and sent to the mainland lost any opportunity for education within the mainstream public education system. If their age was determined accurately, they would have been accommodated with other teenagers and gained the support from Maximus or Life without Barriers, they would also have been treated very differently by Serco, Immigration and IHMS staff, in short, they would have been supported. I was really shocked that the personal impression of a public servant could have such a dangerous and permanent impact on the lives of vulnerable children, it was another example of extraordinary power and responsibility being placed into ill-equipped hands.

Chapter 6

Live Call

Passivity is the same as defending injustice.

Deepak Chopra

Akhtar

The first thing that struck me when I met Akhtar was what a beautiful looking boy he was, he had the most incredible piercing green eyes and dark black hair not unlike the famous Afghan girl *National Geographic* photograph. Akhtar was a fourteen-year-old Afghan boy who had spent two months on his journey to Christmas Island travelling alone through Pakistan, Malaysia and Indonesia. He had been born and raised in Paktia Province Afghanistan and was from a small ethnic tribe, used to a simple lifestyle, the men of his family had worked as shepherds for generations. When Akhtar turned thirteen he started working with his Dad, this was where he met a shepherd girl working the same hills and they started a deadly friendship.

Any liaison, no matter how innocent with the opposite sex was strictly against the local Pashtun law and this girl's brother was a member of the Taliban who took this law very literally. When her brother discovered their friendship, he was incensed with rage and threatened to kill Akhtar to maintain his family honour. Akhtar's father tried to reason with the man, when this failed he offered himself instead of his son. The Taliban took Akhtar's father away, cut his throat, decapitated and mutilated his body and deliberately left his remains on the mountainside to be collected by Akhtar, the girl was the next victim. She was killed as a punishment for committing 'adultery' and dishonouring her family name, the young friends had not even held hands. Akhtar was forced to remain in hiding in the family home for four months until after receiving further death threats a decision was made by his uncle and mother that he must leave the country. His uncle arranged for his travel to Kabul then on to Pakistan where he stayed in Peshawar for twenty-five days, from Pakistan he travelled to Malaysia and Indonesia and by boat to Christmas Island. On Christmas Island every new arrival was granted a phone call referred to as a *live call,* it's the opportunity to contact loved ones to let them know they have survived the journey. When Akhtar made his *live call,* he contacted people from his village and was told that his family had been forced to flee so he had no way of contacting them or knowledge of their whereabouts. When I sat with Akhtar I found myself wondering how this simple shepherd boy managed to travel from the mountainside in Afghanistan to Christmas Island. Just two months prior he had never had a single night away from home, he had never seen the ocean and he was being raised in the traditions of rural Afghanistan prioritising family, tribe, religion first and now here he was so hopelessly alone and scared.

It's the way he bent his index finger of his right hand and bit hard on the knuckle that I will never forget. He was trying so hard not to cry when he looked directly at me with those gorgeous green eyes, his voice was only just above a whisper when he said *I killed my father.* It was then that he bit down on his finger to stop the tears, and an anguished sobbing cry caught us both off guard. I had to force myself from hugging him, the automated desire to rescue still rears up no matter how many heartbreaking encounters I come across and is something all counsellors have to manage particularly at the start of careers. For this beautiful boy the guilt and shame were so immense it was physically and emotionally overwhelming not only for him but for me also. His grief was so intensely raw I felt that it sucked all the energy from the room leaving me to struggle to compose myself and to come up with a meaningful strategy to support him.

To add to his misery, he was socially isolated in the detention centre because he was the only Pashtu unaccompanied minor and was unable to communicate with the other boys. He desperately wanted his mum, his dad, his brothers, sister, grandparents, aunts, uncles, cousins, friends, his old life back. I immediately added Akhtar for discussion at the next meeting to push for him to be transferred into community detention on the mainland where he could be provided the appropriate support from an Afghan Pashtun community. Akhtar needed help to deal with the guilt and self-blame he felt for the death of his father and his friend and for altering the lives of his entire family. He experienced frequent nightmares and flashbacks of his fathers mutilated body and as if that wasn't enough, he was experiencing an immense culture shock. It wasn't rocket science to know that this child needed nurturing with solid supports around him, it was very frustrating to find that it took weeks of combined petitioning from our service, from Life without Barriers and from IHMS to get this kid off the island. When Akhtar was transferred to the mainland I was unable to follow-up with a clinician-to-clinician handover due to the immigration privacy policy this has left me to wonder if he received the care that he so desperately needed. Eight years later I am sometimes haunted by the memory of Akhtar's stunning green eyes and his tragic loss of innocence.

Towards the end of my five years on the island I was asked by a IHMS staffer if I considered myself an advocate or a clinician, I said that I was a clinician first and foremost but that within the role there was a need to advocate for the client as they had very few people willing or able to speak up for them. This woman was in a senior position in IHMS and told me that she had been linked in on a teleconference with Immigration Canberra when I had *really let them have it* she said *I wish I could do that and get away with it like you do Chris.* It certainly highlighted to me how fear driven and intimidating working in the detention system is. Health care professionals carry on with practices and conditions that they would never condone or agree to in another setting and all too often advocating for the clients was seen as radical and obstructive, yet it is the duty both professionally and ethically of any health care worker to advocate for the client. On so many occasions it was left to our little T&T team to write recommendations to IHMS and Immigration in an attempt to prevent further deterioration to a person's mental state. Vulnerabilities are heightened in the detention environment, it's essentially a prison after all, if people arrive in a distressed state it's not the environment to create calm. Sometimes there were simple solutions, for example requesting to send a client into community detention where access to services and community will help to heal, other cases were more complex and we certainly had many reasons to advocate. There are always some cases such as Aktar's that could break my heart, I have prayed for this boy and really hope the prayers are answered.

Habib and Leyla

Another client I spent a huge amount of time and energy advocating for was Habib, or I should say, I advocated on Habib's behalf for his sister Leyla. Habib was a sixteen-year-old boy who had travelled alone all the way from the Al Muthanna province of Iraq. He was the second youngest of five children, sadly two brothers had been missing for four years and his oldest brother Mohammad had been killed during the war but he spoke of them often keeping them alive in his memory. His fourteen-year-old sister Leyla was born with a congenital heart condition and had been receiving medical assistance from the local Italian Military base, however this had ceased when the family were blocked from attending the base by the local militia.

The family had been advised that Leyla's prognosis was poor, she needed cardiac surgery and the family had limited funds and no way to access the surgery. Habib's father had once worked as a security guard but when that work finished up he leased his house out for use as a party reception centre. This has been frowned upon by the local militia as they did not approve of the alcohol and mixed parties, as a consequence the family had been driven from their home and forced to live in a nearby village. The militia group had targeted Habib, severely beating him and slashing his arm and legs with a razor, his family were told that the next time he would not be spared so they were forced to make the hardest decision, to send their only surviving son out to safety. The family remained behind, under threat of attack and Leyla was unable to access her medical care.

Habib had been raised in an active war zone where he had witnessed the death of family and friends, and had in more recent times been badly assaulted, however when we met his primary focus was on his sister Leyla. He loved her very much and he was desperately worried that she would die as she had no further access to medical treatment and the family had no possibility of surgery. I remembered Moira Kelly's *Children First Foundation* in Victoria, they use contacts throughout the medical world to treat children in conflict zones, so I contacted the organisation. Over a series of weeks, I managed to secure medical records scanned and emailed through from Iraq, this was not an easy feat, the family were illiterate and they were in an unsecured area. I had to recruit Habib's school friend back home to take the documents to an internet shop, once I received them I sent them onto *Children First* who sent them through to a cardiac surgeon in India. After the surgeon reviewed the records he accepted Leyla's case, offering to do the surgery at no cost. The foundation offered to pay flights and accommodation for Leyla and her mother to fly from Baghdad to Chennai in India, where Leyla would have the surgery, recuperate and then be returned to Baghdad. I was elated when I finally confirmed it with Habib, we phoned his mother on a couple of occasions and we arranged another call for his next session.

When Habib came into the room I knew something wasn't right, he told me that his mother was unable to get Leyla to Baghdad, that the local militia had made it far too dangerous to travel and they saw no way of accepting the offer of surgery. In the meanwhile, Habib was getting ready to be transferred to Leonora on the mainland, the Department of Immigration had opened up this detention facility in the middle of Western Australia and were sending UAMs and family groups there; we knew he would be sent soon and my communication with him and his family would be badly affected. My euphoria plummeted when after weeks of stalling both the foundation and the surgeon I had to cancel the whole arrangement. By then Habib was in Leonora, we phoned often and he had great workers from Serco and Life without Barriers supporting him, we were all incredibly sad not to see this through. I had to admit the security situation in Iraq was not improving, Habib's family were in a terrible situation and it wasn't about to improve no matter how long I procrastinated before calling off the arrangements. It's difficult for us in Australia to imagine not being able to access a city like Melbourne or Sydney from a country area, especially when the need is so great. These situations are a common reality for people trying to survive in conflict zones, the dangers are very real and there just aren't many happy endings. I eventually lost contact with Habib and have been unable to offer any opportunity to negotiate another attempt at surgery for Leyla. I have hoped that Habib will have kept some of the dialogue we had to maybe get someone else to pick up where I was compelled to stop.

Mohsen: A voluntary return

People are driven by fear and courage in equal measure when they seek asylum, the persecution they are fleeing is not forgotten or resolved when they leave so it was unusual to see people request to be returned home. I was very curious when I received a call one day from the assistant director of client services, she was wondering if I had time to talk to a young Kurdish man who was volunteering to return to Iran. Mohsen had refused to discuss his decision with immigration officials when he requested to be returned to Iran soon after arriving on Christmas Island and being a naturally curious person, I was intrigued to hear his motive and guessed that it would be a tragic one.

I remember him very clearly, he was a handsome young guy roughly twenty-five years of age with black hair trimmed into a short back and sides, his fierce black eyes were levelled straight at me as he said *I have no choice I must go home.* His face was hard and determined and as he sat very rigid and alert in the armchair I could see there was a need in him to share his story but it was to be on his terms, we both knew it would be the only time we would ever meet, this granted him license to be unrestrained and brutally honest.

His troubles began after his family became vocal activists for the Kurdish people, Mohsen and his two brothers had been arrested together, detained and physically and mentally tortured by the authorities. One of the sick games they were forced to endure was to be blindfolded and marched into a courtyard, have a gun put to their heads and told they were about to die, the gun would never fire and the guards would laugh and march them back in the cell. The mental anguish from this is so hard to imagine and yet it gets worse. The brothers experienced this treatment repeatedly over many months until the occasion when Mohsen's blindfold was removed, he was forced to watch his brothers be executed beside him, after this horror the authorities released him.

Understandably Mohsen's parents wanted him safely out of the country before he was taken again, so they pooled their resources and arranged for him to be smuggled out. When he finally arrived on Christmas Island he made his *live call* home and his mother answered the phone. She told him the authorities now had his father and would only release him in exchange for Mohsen. He knew very well that he was returning to certain death, I made sure that we talked about this because I had to know that he had full appreciation and acceptance of the decision he had made. He knew that the likelihood of his father being released was pretty small. He was expecting to be arrested, detained, tortured and eventually killed but he wanted to give his Dad a chance to live. It was one of the most powerful conversations I have ever had, as we talked he became less guarded and relaxed more into the chair, his intense stare diminished and he became warmer and more engaged. He told me that he would never live a free life knowing that he hadn't gone back to try and save the life of his father. I was deeply humbled by his love and sacrifice but it was the discussion about his return to be tortured that stays with me, he gave a satiric grunt and said *they can torture me, what haven't they done to me already.* I was deeply affected by meeting Mohsen, he held such honour and morality something that is not usually exposed on a first meeting.

When I went back to the big board room at Northwest Point and sat down with the CPPM agenda in front of me, Mohsen's name and boat number was still on the list for discussion. He had been returned to Iran the day before to Tehran via Perth, when we got to his boat number the immigration official chairing the meeting simply said, *oh good, we don't need to talk about him, he's a problem solved* and started to discuss the next person. I felt so incensed that my gut momentarily froze, with the heat of my blood rushing up my limbs through to my neck and my ears. I had two thoughts travelling through my mind at once, firstly I wanted each person present to have a very clear understanding of the people they willingly referred to by numbers. And secondly, I wanted to deliver this information in a way that honoured this man's life. I had to work hard to maintain control, as calmly and clearly as I could, I said *let me just tell you about this person. His name is Mohsen and he is not a problem solved.* As I gave a very brief summary of the sacrifice he was making, it became very clear to me that no one in the room knew of his story, the uncomfortable silence was brilliant.

Mohsen is not the only person to have been put in that position however, he is the only person that I met with such a deadly choice. I won't forget him and I can't help wondering if he is dead or alive. His is the only name I have not altered while writing this memoir, I felt changing his name would be dishonourable. This incident in the boardroom is something that also sits with me, it is an excruciating example of the dramatic difference in the agenda of public servants and health professionals, sometimes these differences were just too confronting.

There were others who chose to return because the thought of rotting away on Nauru or on Manus Island was not an option. I met with three young men from Iraq who each chose to return for different reasons. One man returned due to his wife's failing health, he was fearful that she would die before he could gain a protection visa and opted to return to Baghdad to nurse her. One week after the Australian government flew him home the country started spiralling into hell again and I am left to wonder if he survived.

Involuntary deportations

Australia received more than 5,000 Sri Lankan asylum seekers between July and December 2012, this number was considered out of control by the Department of Immigration, Customs and the general public. In response the Gillard government introduced a speedy assessment process called the *Enhanced Screening Process.*[21] The explanation provided was that many of the claims made by Sri Lankan asylum seekers indicated that they were looking for a better life, not necessarily fleeing for their lives and that since the civil war had ended there were no longer any significant problems for a Tamil in Sri Lanka. The department offered assurances that the assessments were to be done in a manner consistent with Australia's *non-refoulement obligations.* Non-refoulement is a principle of international law, which forbids the rendering of a victim of persecution to his or her persecutor, Australia's non-refoulement obligations as a signatory to the 1951 *Convention Relating to the Status of Refugees* prohibit the removal of anyone from Australia to a country where they are in danger of death, torture or other mistreatment, including arbitrary detention.[22]

Using the Enhanced Screening process, each Sri Lankan asylum seeker was offered a brief interview conducted by two immigration workers. An interpreter was made available and people are asked roughly twenty questions to determine if they were allowed to go onto further assessment. If the person was deemed appropriate, he or she was *'screened in'* and could then stay for the process of refugee status determination. But if the immigration workers determined that an individual did not raise claims that engage Australia's non-refoulment obligations then they were *'screened out'* of the protection assessment process and removed from Australia. For obvious reasons this set off alarm bells in our little office and amongst human rights lawyers and the refugee legal centres across Australia. The process of conducting a short interview with people who have just arrived is inherently flawed, particularly when that person is unaware of the impact their answers will have on their claim for asylum. The vast majority of interviews were conducted within hours or days of arrival and some are being conducted on the water to this day. The questions and the interviewers did not account for the significant cultural implications and the impact of trauma on the men, women and children interviewed. For example, I am yet to meet a Tamil who would trust anyone in a uniform. Someone presenting in a uniform gives them a power advantage and immediate authority, this will trigger fear and suspicion in anyone who has been as repeatedly wronged as the Tamil population have by all positions of authority and by every uniform in their homeland. So of course, a uniform will place anyone into a state of heightened fear and suspicion. The Tamils also maintain a cultural politeness that inhibits the ability to describe instances of humiliation, sexual abuse and torture to strangers. I have no doubt that this has led to an enormous number of people simply answering yes or no, providing little or no detail and that they were completely unaware that this flawed interview was the only chance at freedom. I often cringed when a Tamil would tell me they felt safe now they were on Australian soil because *Australians are good people they will protect us,* I didn't have much to say to that.

Enhanced screening assumes that people with real protection concerns will talk about those concerns in a single short interview. Having worked with as many Sri Lankans as I have I can comfortably say that it is very rare for a person to disclose all the traumatic events and exposure to torture and suffering within the first session, and that is when they have been talking to a person without a uniform in a welcoming environment. Obviously, such a discussion needs a build-up of rapport and trust. My other concern is with the validity of the enhanced screening interviews. Once again there is no accountability, the decision is reviewed internally within the Department of Immigration and there is no record of the interview or the decision supplied to the asylum seeker who is *'screened out'*.

Some of our clients started telling us that immigration was giving them a *'choice',* they could sign up with the International Organisation for Migration (IOM) to receive some small monetary support on arrival back in Sri Lanka or stay and wait to be deported. Many chose to sign up with IOM in the hope that signing would delay the process of return and they would avoid being added to an involuntary transfer list. During this wait they desperately tried to engage lawyers but this was not easy. This signed 'agreement' was farcical as they were given no choice, no guarantee of safety from immigration and IOM was unable to confirm that Sri Lanka was safe for return.

I sometimes reflect on the Serco, IHMS, Immigration and AFP staff who escorted the Tamils back to Colombo and wonder what was going on in their mind when they walked each person onto the plane. I wonder if any of these workers ever questioned the legal and moral implications of what they were doing. Since the introduction of the Enhanced Screening Process there have been nearly 2,000 Sri Lankan Tamil, men, women and children involuntarily returned on chartered planes directly from Christmas and Cocos Island and the mainland. Many Tamils sent back from the Cocos Islands were not medically cleared and were not granted the right to seek asylum. My colleagues and I were really affected by the deportations because we were never privy to the information about transfers before they happened, we would hear through a staff connection with someone working in the centre or at the airport of a pending flight. We started checking *Flightchecker* online to monitor when unidentified charter flights were making their way to the island.

When the first deportations happened I was horrified, and felt so incredibly powerless, I started providing Tamil clients with the contact details of the refugee and asylum seeker legal centre and Australian Tamil organisations for support. Contacting lawyers and having clients signed up for legal services initially eased the powerlessness, but not for long. The changes in Immigration policy included new legislation making legal representation impossible and I soon found that there was no way to prevent the deportations. It seemed to me that the principle of non-refoulement was no longer sacred. This legal principle doesn't apply if a person is not a recognised refugee and the asylum seekers were denied access to a refugee status assessment therefore, the Australian government was not deporting refugees, just pesky asylum seekers.

Dinanath

I had counselled enough Tamils to know that the security situation within Sri Lanka is unstable and for many Tamils the country is simply unsafe. In 2011 I met Dinanath, a 37-year-old married father of two boys, he had been raised in the north of the country and went to Jaffna University to study commerce. He was teaching at the Royal Institute in Kilinochchi when the war entered its final months. In May 2009 during the heavy conflict the family was displaced in Mullaitivu and spent days in bunkers sheltering from shelling, from there they were herded into the army camps. Dinanath spoke with great detail, I could see that he was in that moment, relieving the terror and helplessness, he told me that during the seventeenth night in the camp some army officers came to his tent and woke him to arrest him. His two-year-old son Bala was clinging to his leg, there was a lot of shouting and the army officer's rifle discharged, Bala was shot and killed. The army took his son's body *to hide the evidence* and took Dinanath to a prison camp in the middle of the jungle. He was astonished to find that his brother was also being held there, along with approximately 150 other men. They were confined in small dark rooms only being let out each day for food and he was subjected to many beatings and forms of torture. One day Dinanath, his brother and five other men were marched into the jungle, his brother and two other men were told to step forward and he was made to watch as they were shot and executed. Immediately after the execution, a helicopter flew overhead and landed at the prison camp nearby, on hearing this the army officers were suddenly in a hurry to get back to the camp to greet the visiting officials so they marched the surviving men back to the prison camp leaving the three dead men on the jungle floor. Dinanath believes that he was going to be executed on that day if not for the arrival of the helicopter and its guests. He was kept in the prison camp for over twelve months and then a chance meeting took place. An old Sinhalese teaching colleague happened to be visiting the camp in his capacity as a recruited military officer, they saw each other and Dinanath told me *I pleaded with my eyes.* The man offered no acknowledgement of recognition and left but he returned the next day and paid the guards to have Dinanath released. He then took Dinanath to a safe house and arranged with a smuggler to get him out of the country. Dinanath told me that there were still over 100 men imprisoned in this jungle camp and that as far as he was aware the camp was not officially recognised and this was months after the formal end of the civil war. When he arrived on Christmas Island he made contact with his uncle living in the UK, who had managed to find news that Dinanath's wife and son were alive, they were being kept hidden while the army were still looking for him.

The international community, with the obvious exception of Australia called for investigations into reports of war crimes and human rights abuse in Sri Lanka, but little has been done. It seems that if things are left long enough people will soon forget and move onto the next headline. It's not that easy for me, I have been in a very privileged position, to have sat with people like Dinanath and I have learnt of the atrocities still being carried out. When immigration started direct deportations from Christmas Island to Sri Lanka our service was never informed, the first we knew of a missing client was when they failed to show up for a session, we would check the transfer list and sometimes feel heartbroken to find our client's name on a deportation list that had already left for Colombo. There was an expectation from the Department of Immigration that we would move on and forget about our clients, it's pretty hard to forget about real people, people that I have sat with, listened to, cared for and tried very desperately to help. I am offering up these true stories so others will also find it that bit harder to justify bad policy and practice and maybe even make a bit of noise.

Raj

Raj was one of my clients who was deported back to Sri Lanka. As a thirty-year-old he had never known peace. He was from Batticaloa in the north-east of Sri Lanka. His whole family was killed in the war when he was a young boy, and very luckily for him he was taken in by another family. He has very vague memories of his parents, two sisters and one brother. When he was twenty-years-old he left the country to avoid being made to fight in the civil war as the Tamil Tigers were forcibly recruiting young men and women and his adopted family wanted him safe. Raj got a job in Qatar working as an unskilled labourer, however he was returned to Sri Lanka when the company contract ended along with his work visa but he was forced to live in hiding while the LTTE were looking for fighters. Eventually Raj got another contract to work in Dubai where he stayed for six years from 2006 until 2011. He voluntarily returned to Sri Lanka believing that the war had ended and he would be free to start a new life, he soon lived to regret this decision. Raj was immediately faced with flagrant persecution and constant threats to his life and he felt that he had no choice but to flee to safety. His family helped with the arrangements and he boarded an old wooden fishing boat from Sri Lanka in August 2012 with sixty men and women. After three days at sea, the engine failed and the boat with its desperate passengers drifted for seventy-eight days surviving on rainwater and the occasional raw fish. Two men died before they were found and rescued by Indonesian fishermen, they were taken to an Indonesian island where they were detained by authorities in a prison camp.

Being detained in the prison was yet another traumatic experience for Raj and it was during this time that he witnessed three men being beaten to death. The murdered men were Burmese Rohingya Muslims who were targeted by Burmese Buddhists, detained together in a small cell. The ethnic and sectarian differences had nurtured pure hatred between the men which escalated into physical violence, Raj described the brutal killing of the three men as the most gruesome event he had ever witnessed. To add to the horror the prison guards forced Raj to clean the blood from the room the next day, he described being sickened by the ordeal and he said the smell of the blood clung inside his nostrils for days. He escaped the prison ten days later but was recaptured very quickly and returned to the prison where he was held in the cell for weeks and let out only for meals. It wasn't until he was able to contact his family back home that he was able to access money to pay his way out and he made a second attempt by boat to Christmas Island. This time the boat started taking on water but luckily, they were in Australian territorial waters and were rescued by the Australian Navy, however unfortunately with all the delays in his journey by the time he made the trip to Christmas Island the Immigration policy has changed.

I saw Raj on about eight occasions and also took him out on a directed outing with his friends, over this time I watched him become increasingly anxious and fearful of the threat of deportation. He had heard from someone that had been returned and was warned that he would be arrested on arrival. Everyone was afraid of the fourth floor of the Criminal Investigation Department (CID) building in Colombo, the building and the department are infamous among Tamils because it's where practices of torture were performed and was often referenced as a place of fear and dread. It's where Raj was certain he would end up, I watched as his mental state was badly affected by the stress of waiting for notification that he was to be deported. The notification eventually came in December 2013, Raj was deported directly to Colombo and I fear that he did end up on the dreaded fourth floor. I had given him my email address to make contact in the event of deportation but I have not heard from him and he had made a promise that he would be in contact.

Unaccompanied Minors

There were always Unaccompanied Minors (UAMs) arriving on Christmas Island, the youngest I was made aware of was an eleven-year-old Afghan boy, travelling on his very own and three young sisters who inadvertently were separated from their mother in Indonesia. The girls were boarded onto the boat in darkness and their mother was somehow missed in the chaos, they were seven, eight and nine years old and arrived with a boatload of strangers, the journey would have been terrifying for them. The little girls had older siblings on the mainland and eventually were reunited with them, but not before they had endured months of separation from their family and forced detainment on Christmas Island. The Department of Immigration sanctioned a transfer to the mainland but these small kids were made a political example. They had arrived after the introduction of the *No Advantage* policy and all arrivals were told they were not allowed entry to Australia mainland, no matter what the circumstances, this message was repeated at every opportunity. I was told when they were finally sent to the mainland, they were held in community detention housing with carers who would not let them sleep together so when they cried at night they were alone and unable to comfort each other. When they were finally allowed to be reunited with their older siblings they were told that they must agree to be processed under the same terms and conditions as their young sisters, though they had arrived before the reintroduction of regional processing. They are all living together at the moment but their asylum claims are yet to be processed and their mother is stuck in Indonesia. I found it frustrating that these small children were never referred to our service, they received support from the IHMS team however, the trauma of fleeing a homeland, forced separation from family and forced detainment should in my mind, have meant an automatic referral to our service, but this leads to yet another concern I have.

I believe there is an evident conflict of interest in the legal guardianship of UAMs. When unaccompanied children arrive seeking asylum they are granted the legal guardianship of the Minister for Immigration, but the interests of the child cannot be paramount when the interests of government and departmental policy are to be met by the guardian. If the children had an external guardian they would not be as vulnerable to politically motivated exploitation. Children such as the three little girls would have been given a greater opportunity to access supportive services and treatment; they could even have been treated with dignity.

I am not privy to the number of UAMs that arrived in the five years during my time on Christmas Island, but what I can say is that the number of referrals to our service for this extremely vulnerable cohort was in no way reflective of the numbers arriving. We all counselled children but this included children arriving with parents or other family members. There was enough work for a separate child and adolescent service and yet the majority of children were never referred. The kids we did see had been exposed to horror such as Amina, who was severely traumatised after finding the decapitated head of her friend's mother. When she went to visit her girlfriend the Al-Shabab militia had just left after murdering the mother of her friend and ransacking the house. Her friend's mum had deliberately distracted the men to allow her daughter to escape, knowing they had come to claim the girl for their sexual amusement. They used a machete for the beheading and left her head on the door step. These were the traumatic experiences the kids we counselled had endured. Amina was left with this image for life, sometimes no amount of counselling removes something so vivid and horrific.

Naji

Another unaccompanied minor I counselled was sixteen-year-old Naji, he was like all sixteen year old boys, very difficult to get talking but once I won his trust he was open to sharing. Naji was from Iraq, his father had studied a degree in literature and was fluent in the English language however he wasn't able to find work in this field and worked as a builder. Naji started school at a local primary school in 1999 and then the war began in 2001 with the arrival of the American forces, Naji's father was pleased to get employment as an interpreter for the US forces until he started to receive threats.

In 2003 Naji was kidnapped by the Al Mahdi army and held captive for one week, during this time he was tortured, beaten repeatedly over his head and body, had his front teeth knocked out and then had fuel thrown over his body and was set alight. He sustained burns to his upper body, mainly his left arm and across his back, but he was also had some burns to his left leg. He was rescued after one week during heavy fighting and taken back to his family home where his mother dressed his wounds with only access to traditional local medicine. The wounds healed but he has heavy scarring and restricted movement in his left arm. It was after this torture that his father stopped working as an interpreter and the family moved away to live on a rural property with his paternal grandfather. He told me that he enjoyed living on the farm but he had always known that it would be a temporary measure as his parents were terrified and also felt some degree of guilt and shame when they looked at his scars because they had failed to prevent the harm.

Naji missed school during 2003 due to his injuries and he returned to school for just two years then left to work with his father and grandfather on the small farm. He told me that it was not the life his parents wanted for him, they were forced to live each day in fear that the Al Mahdi army would find them so they made a heart breaking decision. They spent their life savings on his passage to Australia and arranged with family friends living in Australia to care for Naji when he arrived. When he described the farewell he was sobbing. He hoped to go to school, get a good job and one day bring his parents to Australia to safety, this was his dream and his purpose. I am sure that his parents hugged and cried with their son at that farewell, not knowing if they would ever see him again.

Travelling as an unaccompanied minor heightens all the threats as they are at risk of every type of abuse and are frequently sexually exploited on the journey. The danger is not over once they get on a boat because this was also a place of great risk and not just of drowning, we had numerous cases where people were raped on the boat. Rani was a sixteen-year-old girl travelling with her two young brothers directly from Sri Lanka, they were on the water for twenty days before being rescued near the Cocos Islands. Rani told me it had been a frightening ordeal because the driver of the boat and several men travelling with them constantly harassed and intimidated her. She was unable to sleep at night due to fear of sexual abuse and was too frightened to tell her brothers of the degree of harassment due to fear of retribution. The men had threatened to throw her youngest brother overboard and she was frightened that this would happen, so she stayed silent. Rani denied they raped her but I wasn't convinced, there was an unspoken language between the siblings that melded shame, protection and honour and they accepted that they had survived and were together.

When I first arrived *Life Without Barriers* held the contract to provide support services and act as independent observers with the UAMs, this changed later to *Maximus Solutions* but the work was the same with the main job being to provide a level of supportive interaction. Having an independent observer present for interviews was considered a worthy task, a safety net for a vulnerable child. Unfortunately there is no legislative requirement for the department to provide an independent observer with every interview conducted with a UAM. There were many interviews conducted unobserved. There was also a genuine concern that many of the observers were intimidated by the process and felt uneasy speaking up on behalf of the children, effectively diminishing the value of being the third person present.

In 2010 eminent psychiatrist Professor Patrick McGorry was announced Australian of the year and in his acceptance speech he said that immigration detention centres are *factories for producing mental illness* and people nodded and agreed with his wisdom. It was nothing new but we were pleased to hear someone so prominent say it out loud. The government at the time flew Professor McGorry to Christmas Island where he received a very controlled and measured tour of the facilities to allay his fears, he even visited my workplace and met with our team. We had a photograph taken with him all standing smiling at the camera, while the immigration chaperons ensured we had no time alone to talk to him and he was whisked out of the building before we could engage in any dialogue. Visits such as these occurred from time to time, with dignitaries granted access to the immigration detention system as a public display of transparency to indicate they had nothing to hide. Of course the reality is that the Department of

Immigration lock people in and do everything they can to keep the public out. The research on the detrimental effect of detainment on people's mental health was completed years ago and we had all supposedly learnt from the dark days of forced detainment. We knew that children should not be detained because it causes enormous harm, Christopher Bowen was the Minister for Immigration in 2010 and he announced that children and families would not spend more than three months in detention. They were to be screened quickly and transferred into the community because it was well documented that detaining children is abhorrent. We were relieved because the conditions for the families held on Christmas Island were shocking and made even worse by the fact that 2010 had been an exceptionally wet year, this meant very little access to play areas. The crowded covered walkways between the demountable buildings of CC were the only accessible play area for hundreds of children and it was woefully in adequate. It is now 2018 and children remain incarcerated indefinitely on Nauru, in conditions described by the United Nations Committee Against Torture as *cruel, inhumane, and unlawful* I am left wondering just when our nation will act to prevent harm to the most vulnerable.

Chapter 7

We Broke Them

Freedom is the open window through which pours the sunlight of the human spirit and human dignity.

Herbert Hoover

Adel and Ehsan

In 2011 I met Adel and Ehsan, the two men had fled Iran together after refusing to train the Guardians of the Revolution in martial arts. Adel was a black belt karate expert and the coach of the Iranian national team, when the Iranian authorities wanted to employ him he refused, they initially left him alone but they came calling again and this time they wanted his best student as well, this was Ehsan. They both refused to train the authorities and then the threats began, their families were monitored and directed to convince the men to accept the job but they also refused. Consequently, the men were arrested, imprisoned and badly beaten and when they were released they received warnings that the treatment was to continue until they agreed to train the authorities so they decided to leave the country.

When I discovered Adel's passion for karate and just how good he was I asked if he could give an exhibition to the community. This gave him a drive, he was excited to be showing off his skills and I organised an event at the community recreation centre. Adel and Ehsan had brought their official Iranian karate uniforms with them which were being held in the property department in NWP, so I arranged to have them released and I picked them up and cleaned and ironed them with great care, ready to wear. On the day of the performance I picked the guys up as a *directed outing,* when I met them they were concerned their performance would be pretty average because Serco had told them they were not allowed to chop any wood in half because it was going to be too dangerous. These guys were professionals who had been training and practicing Karate for years and they wanted the chance to show their stuff. I took the guys to the hardware shop and bought some wood, we went to the rubbish tip to gather some extra props and to the beach to collect large rocks because they wanted to show how they could snap these in half too. I am chuckling as I write this, recalling how I smuggled the wood and rocks through the back door of the recreation centre to bypass the Serco staff, I enlisted a friend who worked at the recreation centre to help set up and the guys were fabulous, no injuries and most importantly they felt respected.

Adel and Ehsan's reasons for seeking asylum were identical but after waiting for months for the outcome of their refugee status assessments Adel was recognised as a refugee and Ehsan was rejected. Adel was devastated, he felt solely responsible for his student and he blamed himself for the mess they were in, up until this point Adel had been continuing to train Ehsan with a very strict regime that incorporated diet, exercise and discipline. Ehsan responded very well to this and it helped him cope with the separation from his family and the stress of detainment. Adel was always immaculately groomed, he was a real presence in a room and people noticed when he walked in because he was distinguished. He encouraged other men in detention to maintain a routine and to remain hopeful, so he was well known and admired.

After Ehsan received the rejection, I watched Adel's mental state slowly deteriorate, he found the conditions in detention untenable and the roles reversed with Ehsan supporting him. For a man that was usually well groomed, he would arrive to sessions unshaven and unkempt, he was hardly sleeping and when he did he had horrific nightmares. He also struggled with immense guilt and shame that his student was suffering and also that his student was now supporting him. When once he sat with a regal presence, he now slumped in the chair struggling to make eye contact. He became quick to anger, especially when it had been six months since his refugee status was granted and he was still waiting for the security check. He also became socially withdrawn and stopped training and lost a dramatic amount of weight, he looked gaunt, with little energy and was very depressed. IHMS offered anti-depressants, which he was reluctant to take, he disclosed that he was having suicidal thoughts and I worried that he would act on them. I kept hounding his immigration case manager for the update on his security clearance and was told that because he had travelled to several countries with the Iranian karate team his security clearance was more complex. ASIO wanted to make sure that he was visiting each country purely as a karate coach and not as an Iranian spy or would-be terrorist.

Eventually the two guys were transferred together to the mainland where they had to continue waiting in another detention facility for several months. During this time I managed to make phone contact with Adel in an attempt to keep his hope alive because he was pretty depleted by then. Ehsan's suffering was also made even harder when Adel made a significant attempt to end his own life. He was eventually granted a positive security clearance and they both received permanent visas but not before the process broke them.

When I first arrived on Christmas Island, I naively assumed that all people detained would be treated with some humanity and compassion, it didn't take long to discover this was far from reality. There were so many occasions when my colleagues and I would just roll our eyes because some of the practices by Serco and immigration staff were just ludicrous and it seemed to me that good old-fashioned common sense didn't enter the equation too often. With Immigration staff I found there was often a callous lack of humanity, for example, I remember taking a phone call from one of the immigration assistant directors at Northwest Point, she told me that the department was transferring a young man to Manus Island in the morning, he had arrived with his mother but they were accommodated separately and he was being treated as a single adult male. She said *we think that his mother is going to be a bit upset when she finds out that he's been transferred, could you see her?* When I asked the logical question; *Why transfer him away from his mother?* She didn't have an answer, other than state he was here *illegally* and was going to be subject to the same treatment as everybody else. I asked if she was going to allow a final farewell, she said *no, if we let that happen things might get out of hand.* I was horrified, as were some of the IHMS staff, when they were directed not to inform the boy's mother when she asked where he was. She was missing her son terribly and asked for regular visits and she was being ignored until immigration saw fit to inform her. Our service was used at times to cover people's tracks, to tick a box to ensure that when this shameful period is scrutinised in the future, it would be considered that the wellbeing of people was addressed by allowing access to a counselling session. I still don't know why this young man was singled out for transfer to Manus Island, his transfer had the potential to separate a family for the rest of their lives. These heartless decisions made by public servants were senselessly adding misery upon misery.

Another practice that I found bizarre was that when people arrived in their sad and sorry state on the island, all their belongings were taken from them en masse. There was no accurate record taken of whose medication belonged to whom and important aids like eyeglasses and hearing aids were frequently lost and destroyed. We would see people who had been medicated for years for a variety of medical complaints and would often find that they had their regular medication ceased on arrival. When I asked the logical question *why did you stop taking your medication* I received a response that *it was taken off me and they haven't given it back yet.* There seemed to be a sanctioned use of reactive medicine, in this instance waiting until someone experienced a seizure from sudden medication withdrawal before offering treatment.

There were also the times when our service would occasionally receive a referral from IHMS that was ridiculous, for example, there was the referral for the deaf-mute client who no one could communicate with, how were we suddenly going to provide counselling to a man with no verbal or sign language available? Then there was the young man with an acquired brain injury (ABI) with all the predicted behaviours associated with an ABI, so he was undoubtedly a handful within the detention environment, because he should not have been detained. I assumed the people making the referrals wanted our service to help petition to have the clients transferred off island to access appropriate care, but I wasn't always convinced. There was also the vital need for our service to advocate for families to remain together for the birth of a child or when they were sent off island for significant medical treatment but I found it extraordinary that I was forced to put energy into begging the Department of Immigration to keep families intact. I still find it astounding that it was considered acceptable to separate children, babies and families for months at a time. I am not talking about a few days, people were sent to the mainland for treatment or to deliver their babies and they did not return for weeks or months.

And yet another example of the ridiculous was Serco's attempt at facilitating a social outing. Christmas Island has a wonderful outdoor cinema open each Saturday night, sometimes Serco would bring along a minibus of asylum seekers from the family camp at Construction Camp or Phosphate Hill. The problem was that Serco didn't bother to check the details of the film and would often bring kids and family groups to inappropriate films. I remember watching *The Girl with the Dragon Tattoo* which was rated MA and I hated it because I found it graphic and disturbing. I looked across the cinema grounds to see a young girl that I had been counselling who had been a victim of severe sexual abuse and there she was brought along to watch a rape scene. It was so unnecessary and disrespectful, it should have been common sense to check a film rating. The details were put into the Christmas Island community newsletter and the cinema club has a website, there were town blackboards advertising the movies and their ratings each week, so it really wasn't hard to ensure a film was appropriate.

One of the truly miserable aspects of working with detained people, is watching a decline in their mental state, people were gradually broken by the length of detainment, particularly someone with a history of incarceration and abuse. The detention environment heightened any trauma symptoms and made the most resilient person question their own sanity at times. I helplessly watched some very strong people fall apart with my only access to help through the Department of Immigration Client Placement and Preventative Meeting (CPPM) process but our recommendations had to be repeated numerous times before we saw any action, if at all. The meetings were held weekly, so if there was a client who needed to be transferred off the island we would start the process by adding them to the CPPM agenda, present the case and then re-schedule the client for follow up counselling and support, knowing that the weeks would pass by before a possible transfer happened. We never made promises to clients, but they placed huge trust and hope in our ability to petition for them and we often felt helpless and would despair over the inadequate process. One person I recall petitioning for was beautiful little Kumaran, a seven-year-old boy who experienced the trauma of witnessing his mother being blindfolded and taken by authorities while his father had a gun held to his head. His mother was returned to the family but not before she had been gang raped and beaten, the family fled from Sri Lanka straight after this. Kumaran was hyper-vigilant and struggling to sleep but when he did sleep he had frightening nightmares and his symptoms were heightened in the detention centre. This child just should not have been detained and yet he was detained for months.

It was not uncommon to find that adult men were so heavily traumatised that they started bed-wetting, in psychiatry this is called nocturnal enuresis.

The symptom is only successfully treated when a client's anxieties can be decreased to a manageable level and obviously this couldn't be achieved in a detention centre. The response from IHMS was to medicate, however the medication can only be prescribed by a psychiatrist and they only visited once a month and even when prescribed, the medication was not guaranteed to work. It had more side effects and potential complications than other medications. Men would be humiliated by the problem and if it was discovered by others, which happened in shared dormitories, they were publicly shamed. We saw other symptoms of psychological distress develop, such as teeth grinding, stuttering, uncontrolled tremors and people pulling the hairs off their bodies, for example eyebrows and arm hair. These were psychological expressions of anxiety and their heightened distressed state which all developed after their arrival onto the island.

Some referrals came through when the client had already been broken and for other clients we watched them gradually declined before our eyes. The breaking down of a person's spirit is done incrementally, it's the little things such as denying access to the internet or the telephone so there is no communication with the outside world. Many people arrived on the island with loved ones in perilous situations and they desperately wanted updates to hear the voice, offer comfort over the phone, and probably make promises they couldn't keep. Other ways to disempower were to not inform people of appointments, by waking people with a demand they should follow without explanation. We often had clients arrive completely unaware they were there for a counselling session, they would arrive with no knowledge of our service or that the referral had been made on their behalf. We would spend half our time calming people, assuring them that we were not working for the police or immigration and that we weren't going to punish them in some way. For many Tamils in this situation the journey to our service could be made worse by the fact they were directed into the small white mini vans used by Serco, the same vans used by the militia groups and people in authority back in Sri Lanka. Often in Sri Lanka when a Tamil climbed into a white van they disappeared for good or were returned after detainment and torture. This became a very common problem for us as we had people arrive in a heightened state of anxiety but it could have been avoided with decent communication. We eventually placed laminated translated information about our service into the Serco transport vans, hoping to allay the client's fear on transportation to our service.

The other disconcerting practice in just the last couple of years, was Serco staff filming clients in the van. Serco officers were directed to use a handheld camcorder to film any client with a high security rating while the client was transferred to our service. A high security rating is granted following an incident of self-harm, aggression or a suicide attempt and the rating will stay in place for weeks until reviewed and lifted. Once again it was Serco using the correctional system to enforce order, this ensured that people who were already in such a distressed state to have attempted to end their life, were kept in that distressed state. Something I felt very disturbed by was that Serco gained more income from the management of clients with a medium to high security rating, therefore there was little incentive to reduce a rating and there was no external monitoring of the rating system to ensure that it was fair. The filming was intrusive, because it was done by an officer sitting directly in front, just a metre away and aiming the camera on the person for the entire drive. When I suggested they could use a mounted camera to reduce the level of intrusion, my recommendation was ignored. It was clear that the intimidation was deliberate, this had such a negative impact on some clients, that we had people decline appointments until the filming stopped.

One of the observations I made was that many clients changed their character while in detention, some men who were normally polite and kind became intolerant and hardened, the detainment had a terrible ability to alter a spirit. Amir was one of my clients I saw for months, he gradually became so frustrated with the length of time for processing and what he perceived as unjust treatment that he felt driven to behave badly. He threw what he described as a tantrum by throwing a rubbish bin and plastic chairs and making a big disturbance in an effort to be heard. He felt so frustrated by the system and this affected his mood terribly, he became clinically depressed and anxious, needing medication to give him some relief. He was one of many in the same situation who were deteriorating day by day and to cap this off, he was granted a higher security rating by Serco further affecting his mood and treatment.

To counsel people in such oppressive circumstances is hard, it's often one step forward two back and we had to be inventive at times to instil hope. I would encourage clients to be creative, to journal their stories and their dreams, to write poetry, paint, draw, sing, dance, exercise, do whatever they possibly could to keep going. Some clients took to this immediately, others had been drained of any creative energy and were lucky to get out of bed to attend a session.

Chapter 8

Breaching Human Rights

Our lives begin to end the day we become silent about things that matter.

Martin Luther King Snr

Matthew and Vani

Matthew had arrived directly from Sri Lanka with significant health problems after being wounded by shelling during the conflict. His left lower leg had been amputated back home in Sri Lanka in a rudimentary hospital during the final days of war, three years prior to his trip to Christmas Island. He had been fitted with a prosthetic limb, however the limb was in need of replacement because it was ill fitting and difficult to walk on. To make matters worse, when he had been injured in the shelling he had sustained serious injuries to the hip and thigh of his *'good'* leg and was in chronic pain. He was travelling with his wife Vani who was suffering with a severe mental illness and so his focus was predominantly on her wellbeing.

Our service did not receive a formal referral for Matthew and Vani, their referral was initiated by me after I had met them at the Catholic

Church. They chatted to me in the lush green gardens of the church yard after a Sunday service, when I said I worked for the health service, it was Vani who begged for help to get a new prosthesis for her husband. I wrote down their names and boat numbers and created a referral, Matthew was walking on ill-fitted crutches that had rubbed his skin raw and caused an open sore in his armpit. He had asked the International Health and Medical Service (IHMS) repeatedly for assistance, however he was told that he would need to wait, a new prosthesis was not a priority and he should be grateful for the crutches. This young couple had arrived after the re-introduction of regional processing so they were fearful that they would be transferred to Nauru or to Manus Island and that in so doing they would not receive the health care they desperately needed. What I found was that clients often put up with pain and discomfort because they were frightened that requesting and appearing needy may end in a transfer or for a Tamil a forced deportation.

Matthew was eventually sent to Darwin for treatment after waiting several months. He was sent without his wife and she predictably experienced a severe deterioration in her mental state which was made worse by the separation, a prediction I had made very clear to the Department of Immigration. Vani was flown to Perth for an acute psychiatric admission and her husband was transferred across the country from Darwin to be with her on recommendations from the admitting psychiatrist. They were returned to Christmas Island together but Matthew's prosthesis had not been replaced, just patched up and it still aggravated the pain from his sore hip, thigh and lower back. The treatment he had received in Darwin had included a scan, investigating his troubled hip and thigh and the outcome wasn't great. The scans found extensive shrapnel causing nerve damage and pain, there was a need for further surgery however, it was delicate and dangerous due to the risk it could potentially lead to the loss of use in his *'good leg'*.

Matthew was resigned to the fact that he would not be offered this surgery while detained but he didn't complain, so I did. Even his accommodation was inappropriate, he was expected to hop in and out of a slippery shower on one leg. This proved to be dangerous, resulting in a few tumbles before Serco offered a change of room to a donger with a shower large enough to accommodate a shower chair. Matthew was so polite and grateful, but how ridiculous and frustrating it was to have to write clinical recommendations to facilitate these requests. I kept wondering why IHMS didn't take his concerns seriously and petition on his behalf. Joint advocacy with the two health care services had the potential to be very successful helping Matthew and so many like him. Unfortunately, I learnt that questioning authority is hard and that speaking out is harder and as the years passed I noticed health care professionals from IHMS were less likely to be a voice for vulnerable people.

IHMS have the contract to provide the medical care to asylum seekers in immigration detention networks in Australia, Manus Island and Nauru. IHMS is essentially a business focussed on profit and I believe there is always going to be ethical conflict when health care is provided alongside a strong business model and motive. Staff are often expected to work in conditions and under circumstances where they feel ethically conflicted and in other settings they would not normally accept such constraints. A contract with IHMS comes with a confidentiality clause, you either put up or get out and you definitely shut-up. Many people found the work way too challenging and distressing, however they were easily replaced with people who would willingly remain silent. What is of great concern to me, is that over the period of five years I observed healthcare professionals become complacent in their duty of care to their clients through an insidious dismantling of health standards. This was initially done in a gradual manner that was explained away as needing to cope with the sheer number of asylum seekers arriving. But over time it became blatant when IHMS accepted directives from the Department of Immigration, directives which, if made on the mainland affecting the Australian populace would have seen everyone '*down tools*'. This documented disregard for safe and standard practice in the healthcare of people seeking asylum has been allowed because IHMS and the Department of Immigration embraced and nurtured the belief that desperate people should be grateful for what they are given. When I worked in Iran, we were working with Afghans that had fled directly over the border with nothing, they were in crisis and we delivered a field response, however IHMS were operating clinics on Australian soil, in conditions not driven by crisis, yet they continued to deliver care as if they were in the field. A field response and an established clinic response are very different, the detention environment was not a target in a war zone, it was not a make shift tent, yet the philosophy behind the care delivery was makeshift, for five long years. I acknowledge there were times that the boat arrivals continued for days, but both IHMS and the government had the time and resources to provide medical care on a par with the general population of Australia and they made a deliberate choice not to.

Of course, not all IHMS clinicians were heartless, some worked with compassion and really cared for the clients, the others cashed in, mortgages were paid off and holidays booked. IHMS staff had to comply with the expectations of their employer and of the Department of Immigration one of the tasks was to sign off on *fit to fly's*. Each person on Christmas Island had to be medically checked and declared fit to fly before being flown off the island. Prior to the re-introduction of the Regional Processing Centres (RPCs) on Nauru and Manus Island a fit to fly was a simple routine procedure done without issue. In fact, when clients told me they had just had a fit to fly I got excited for them because it meant they were a step closer to getting the permanent visa. My excitement plummeted when the Department of Immigration started putting together transfer lists to send people to either Manus Island or Nauru.

IHMS had a representative on the transfer committee and this was normally the chief medical officer and often a mental health representative. The transfer committee looked at the evidence provided by IHMS to ensure that someone is fit to fly, the information was drawn from basic medical assessments and any additional medical reports from illnesses treated while detained. It was also necessary for a mental health assessment, to show there is no immediate impediment to prevent a person flying. Essentially the IHMS representatives had the power to send a person to Manus or Nauru or to be deported to their country of origin, this is where medical staff faced a huge ethical dilemma. When the RPCs were re-opened in 2013 Immigration introduced a fast track assessment system, as no processing of asylum claims was to be done on Christmas Island, so the Department of Immigration wanted to get people off to Nauru and Manus Island or the Tamils back to Sri Lanka as fast as possible. The boats were still arriving and pressure was on to declare people fit to fly and send them on their way and the IHMS staff were directed to comply. Some staff refused to sign off on the assessments but there were more than enough willing participants.

For the majority of my time on the island our service had a good rapport with the IHMS mental health team. We found that if we went out to NWP and met with the team every now and then it helped keep the network open for better quality referrals and an understanding of who we were and how we operated. For a period of time there was an IHMS psychiatrist who visited once a month and he would hold an in-service for the staff which we were invited to on a few occasions. At the time of the fast track assessments, he was obviously struggling with an ethical dilemma because he was trying to provide adequate care to a mentally ill patient and the Department of Immigration was being obstructive. He chose this day to discuss ethical dilemmas and the fact that IHMS were conducting assessments and providing treatment without informed consent. The room was full and it was an incredible discussion to witness, more than half the room failed to grasp the concept that they could challenge authority over patient care. They showed a level of ignorance that I found frightening, when the topic of the fast track assessments was raised, people said they didn't have a problem with doing them and they clearly didn't understand those that did. On the topic of consent, some clinicians misunderstood completely and one nurse said *so are you telling us that you want us to tell the clients what to say,* implying that the psychiatrist was telling them to coach the clients. It was a debacle and it was also a great eye opener, we saw that less than half the IHMS staff shared the same ideology as us. I was left to wonder how it was that I had received the same exposure to working with people with a mental illness as many of the IHMS staff and yet we viewed our work and our clients so differently. I was left ashamed that so many mental health nurses willingly complied with orders that were ethically and morally abhorrent to me.

Another great concern to us was the lack of understanding among the IHMS general medical staff and more disturbingly among the mental health staff, of the effects and management of psychological trauma. IHMS provided all the mental health assessments, access to a visiting psychiatrist, and referrals to our service for clients that had been exposed to torture and trauma. There was a constant flow of referrals to our service but there was a real lack of knowledge among the staff of the impact of detainment on a person with severe trauma exposure. The all too common mistake made was that people were *managed for behavioural issues* because they appeared to be acting out or exhibiting disruptive behaviour. Many of these clients were merely reacting to the detention environment and the negative impact this was having on them. With many of our clients, there was a decreased ability to self-regulate emotions and behaviours when under stress and this sometimes looked like they were deliberately causing a drama. And there were occasions when the medical staff demonstrated negligence. Bishaaro was a sixteen-year-old unaccompanied minor housed in CC, when she became physically unwell with diarrhoea and vomiting she collapsed and was carried to the IHMS clinic within the compound. The medical staff administered a medication to prevent the vomiting but when she developed an allergic reaction to the drug it was ignored and dismissed. She experienced involuntary muscle movement known as tardive dyskinesia and a oculogyric crisis which is an adverse reaction causing a person's eyes to roll uncontrollably. Bishaaro was not believed, because her best friend had been transferred to Darwin for medical reasons at this time, the nursing staff accused Bishaaro of fabricating an illness to join her friend, they thought she was a behavioural issue. Because she was not believed she started to doubt her own sanity, the movements of her arms, legs and eyes were so strong that she had no control over them, yet she was scolded for not stopping the movement. Bishaaro told me that the nurses yelled at her and she was led to believe she was going insane. Four years later, when she was settled on the mainland she was administered the same drug, she experienced the same reaction and it was established that she has an allergy to the drug. Bishaaro contacted me to talk about the experience, she was very upset with the treatment she received on Christmas Island, she said: *They made me think that I was going crazy, that I was mad, why did they do that to me? They were supposed to look after us.*

I recall attending another IHMS in-service that focussed on the topic of *managing* difficult clients, there was a nurse in the room who said sometimes *I just want to slap them*. When a person presenting with behavioural symptoms is supported properly progress can be made, unfortunately with frequent changes in staffing and a poor level of understanding, these clients were generally mismanaged. Being mismanaged in a detention centre can have dire consequences, at NWP it meant being sent to the *'behavioural unit'* which was just a miserable compound with far more security and less activity. Or to *'Red Compound'* which is an imposing box of reinforced steel the equivalent to being sent to a maximum-security prison cell. Being sent there meant that a person's security rating was increased and made a transfer due to a deteriorating mental state nearly impossible. We would present a case at the CPPM with recommendations to transfer a client with severe trauma symptoms into community detention on the mainland. The recommendations reflected the best practice guidelines for T&T survivors endorsing the need for a traumatised person to be housed in a less restrictive environment. It would have been a lot easier for the clients and us, if

IHMS staff had a better understanding of the management of complex trauma symptoms and if they, with this understanding, supported our recommendations and recognised the negative implications of detainment on the health and wellbeing of trauma clients, but often they didn't.

I also recognised that IHMS staff could be incredibly cautious and anxious which is not a very reliable combination, because fear can alter a clinician's judgement. This isn't helped by the fact that working on Christmas Island, in the detention environment was almost like existing in a bizarre alternate universe and situations that you would never accept or abide on the mainland were presented frequently. The Department of Immigration implements a strong model of intimidation, so that people find themselves accepting unsafe, unfair and unethical practices due to fear. Fear of losing your job and being prosecuted for breaching confidentiality is a constant threat that is emphasised repeatedly. There is also the fear of losing professional credibility and it's this level of intimidation that alters clinical judgement.

Many of the IHMS staff took the contract because they just wanted to see for themselves what was going on. The doctors rotated through on short three-week contracts and many just did the one contract and never wanted to return. Others used the rationale that although what they were confronted with was often inhumane, when they were working they provided good care. Others arrived to increase their self-importance, some people that stayed had the biggest of egos that needed to be massaged regularly, the higher up the chain, the greater the power and people thrived on that. The problem with so many coming and going is there is no continuity of care, one doctor would tell a client one thing, another doctor would tell them something else. The clinics were just that, a clinic, where only the basics were provided, medications prescribed and bandages given out. Anything serious was looked at by IOTHS such as the cardiac arrests, the unstable pregnancies, the early labours, the babies with chest infections, severe asthma, infections of every kind, the floridly psychotic and the list goes on and on.

I have mentioned IHMS to some refugees who have been through the system of detainment and they have nothing but praise for the kindness shown by the nurses and doctors. Once again, it's all relative to the individual's story, ultimately if people feel validated they walk away satisfied, the biggest complaints came from clients who felt that no one listened. They worried that their suffering was being ignored and often thought their case was forgotten when the waiting time for access to treatment off island kept extending. They also complained that the common IHMS treatment for any illness was to be told to drink plenty of water and take a Panadol, clients would say *water and Panadol that's all they give.*

I am by no means alone in my concerns over the healthcare provided within the detention system, other healthcare professionals have highlighted their concerns for the lack of humanity provided within the centres. In December 2013 a ninety-two-page document made headlines, it was written by a group of fifteen doctors who had all worked on Christmas Island. In the letter of concern they described a fundamental conflict of interest between their employer, IHMS and the Department of Immigration and Border Protection (DIBP). They wrote: *We have concerns that decisions made by IHMS regarding the provision of care to patients have been compromised by their relationship with the DIBP. As a result, these decisions are not always in the best interest of the patient.*[23] What they described was a list of unsafe, unethical and inhumane practices they felt compelled to abide by. They were genuinely concerned for the clients and also that their own professional registrations may be in jeopardy. They stated: *it is of concern that practitioners working within IHMS may be putting any registration they have with AHPRA* [Australian Health Practitioner Regulation Agency] *at risk by participating in unethical conduct and in gross departures from clinical standards.*

There is a legitimate reason the document is ninety-two pages in length because the number of concerns raised is immense. For example, directing medical staff to conduct pre-departure assessments is fair however, having the time frame reduced to conduct assessments within forty-eight hours of arrival is completely unreasonable. This meant that simple blood tests were abandoned because Immigration was not willing to wait for the pathology results. *In regards to TB (Tuberculosis) screening, all abnormal chest x-rays and reports required review by a TB specialist, prior to patients being declared fit for transfer. Transfer practices in June 2013 reflected these guidelines. However, with increasing pressure from the DIBP to improve processing time, these standards were abandoned.* The direct result of this change in process saw people with active Tuberculosis transferred to Manus Island and Nauru when they were not only unwell but also at risk of infecting large populations. I could go on but I think the point is clear, the doctors revealed a practice of substandard treatment that was being driven by immigration, but condoned by IHMS.

In July 2014 Dr Peter Young, the former IHMS Director of Mental Health Services was compelled to give evidence at the National Inquiry into children in immigration detention. Dr Young was the most prominent health care professional to speak out against the forced detainment and the subsequent psychological damage this is doing to children and adults. He is the most distinguished because of his length of service with IHMS, which was just under three years in the role as Director of Mental Health Services. His evidence has not been disputed, nor has it brought about change, my hope is that with a barrage of evidence, reports and open discussion we can affect change. Some clients were made to go through a protracted ordeal on Christmas Island and I feel that if IHMS had agreed to advocate for clients more actively with us we could have brought about better client outcomes.

Access to basic human rights is something that everyone who seeks asylum is searching for however, what I have witnessed is the further withdrawal of these rights from the most vulnerable of people. When the Gillard government re-opened the Regional Processing Centres, they put in place the *No Advantage* policy that affected thousands of people. I have watched as basic human rights have been stripped away, with forced deportations, indefinite detainment, separation from family members, sexual abuse and deaths all clearly documented.

When people were sent to the mainland on bridging visas with no work rights, they were expected to find housing and survive on $220 per week. The main cities now have little ghettos of Afghan, Iraqis and Iranians all forced to live in squalor because they are unable to work and provide for their children. I distinctly recall meeting with Red Cross caseworkers in Perth and inquiring after the amount of support provided to people when they were released into the community. I was told that after six weeks of support the person was expected to survive unassisted and that the Department of Immigration did not consider that homelessness was criteria to extend the support. Understandably workers struggled with this lack of regard for humanity. The Red Cross lost the funding completely in 2014 and hundreds of support services were diminished to bare bones by the current Department of Immigration and Border Protection. Now in 2018 we are re-entering an era of enforced pain and sustained suffering by providing Temporary Protection Visas (TPVs) and the newly introduced Safe Haven Enterprise Visas (SHEVs), these will grant either three or five-year visas with no opportunity for family reunification. The TPV well documented as the cause of severe enduring mental illness has been rebirthed for political gain only and the distress of my clients and thousands of other asylum seekers continues.

Sevvi

One young girl I wonder about often is Sevvi, she was twenty-two years of age when I received her referral from IHMS. She had survived the Sri Lankan civil war, during which she had faced the disappearance of her father, the death of her brother, family displacement and a life in constant fear. Her mother entrusted her fate to Sevvi's maternal uncle and his pregnant wife and they set off from Sri Lanka on a small crowded fishing boat with limited supplies arriving twenty-six days later on Christmas Island. There were hundreds of families in detention at the time and space was limited so the family were placed in temporary accommodation across the road from Construction Camp, in rooms with small bathrooms built into them. Travelling on the same boat was a young unaccompanied minor who was invited by the family to sleep in their room. The boy had been allocated a room to himself but was frightened to be alone, so the uncle and pregnant aunt, their three-year-old daughter, the young unaccompanied boy and Sevvi were all sleeping in the same small room.

During the night Sevvi woke and decided to use the toilet next door in the unused bedroom to prevent waking the others but when she slipped into the toilet she realised she wasn't alone, her uncle had followed her in. He grabbed her by the throat, threw her to the ground and held his hand over her mouth while he raped her. She was so shocked that she didn't scream or raise the alarm at all and she silently returned to her bed and waited until morning. It was one day later when she disclosed what had happened to her, when she was found crying by another female passenger off their boat. The woman promptly went to the IHMS clinic and found the nurses to attend to Sevvi's medical needs and medical staff alerted immigration staff and the AFP. The AFP interviewed Sevvi offering her assurance that her uncle would be charged and punished and the Department of Immigration immediately separated the family, from that point on Sevvi was treated as a single adult female (SAF).

I received the referral not long after this because Sevvi was not engaging with the IHMS staff and they referred her in the hope that our service could support her. Meeting for the first time in my small office her big brown eyes looked startled as she stared at me, taking in the surroundings and checking for safety. She sat opposite me on the white floral two-seater couch, a very petite girl who looked much younger than her years, this was aided by the fact that her dress was about two sizes too big and hanged off her small frame highlighting her extreme vulnerability. She was sobbing, her narrow shoulders heaved as she shared her story of both horror and betrayal, it was incredibly painful for her but she was insistent that she wanted to give all the details. To be honest I truly hate the details, because they allow me to see the person in front of me under attack, to witness the horror through their words. It's an uncomfortable and distressing situation to find myself in at times, the trauma counsellor who doesn't really want to hear the details of the client's trauma.

To add to her distress, she had become the victim of gossip among the Tamils within detention, with many of them siding with her uncle as he denied any wrongdoing. Sevvi told me that she had been a virgin and was now too *'unclean'* to marry. Her grief was huge because she had been abused by a man she had trusted and loved, when Sevvi told her mother what had happened it caused a great rift in the family. Some family members back home blamed Sevvi and declared that she must have seduced him. Sevvi was left confused and damaged by the scandal in the family however her mother remained very supportive even if she was in Sri Lanka.

Sevvi started to ask after the justice process and when I enquired on her behalf I was surprised to hear from immigration that the case was closed due to the lack of evidence. This was ludicrous, I enquired after the AFP report, but was told this was absolutely none of my business. I asked what legal advice or representation Sevvi had been offered, and discovered she had been offered none, so I arranged for a very generous criminal barrister to talk to Sevvi, we set up phone meetings in my office and she accepted her case. This was all very clandestine because Immigration would have hauled me over the coals had they known I was seeking legal counsel for one of the *'detainees'*. By this stage the level of secrecy and monitoring had escalated among the immigration workforce and I decided we could not trust the immigration funded interpreters to be discrete, I started to use a separate phone interpreting service for any legal advocacy. Sevvi's lawyer requested the police and medical reports but we didn't see justice played out. I have learnt that there are few true coincidences when dealing with the Department of Immigration and breaches of humanity, so unsurprisingly within a short period of time Sevvi was transferred to Nauru without any warning. To my knowledge her uncle has never been prosecuted and I am unsure if Sevvi remains on Nauru or has been deported to Sri Lanka. What I do know for certain, is that immigration acted without due process and with a total disregard for Sevvi's human rights, and that is bloody shameful.

Covering up rape within the detention network is not news because we have all been made aware of the atrocities happening in Manus Island and Nauru. The riot that saw twenty-three-year-old Reza Barati beaten to death by the men paid to protect him and the inadequate treatment for an infection, that caused the death of twenty-four year old Hamid Kehazaei were headlines for days and yet we continue to hear people demonised. The few families finally released into a miserable life on Nauru have been offered just $1.50 an hour to pack shelves and are portrayed as ungrateful even when offered a transfer to a poverty stricken underdeveloped nation such as Cambodia. And when the Australian Human Rights Commission released their report *The Forgotten Children* (24) detailing 233 assaults involving children and 33 incidents of reported sexual assault, with the majority involving children the outcry wasn't focussed on the children it was on the hideous vilification of the Human Rights Commissioner Gillian Triggs, what a masterful diversion.

In 2014 Philip Moss the former Integrity Commissioner was instructed by the Abbott Government to investigate allegations of sexual assault on Nauru and to clarify allegations that *Save The Children* workers had assisted with protests and coached people to self-harm in order to generate public sympathy for their plight. The findings of the investigation were released in March 2015 in *The Moss Report.*[25] The independent review backfired on the government and found no conclusive evidence of wrongdoing by the *Save the Children* staff and evidence that at least two women had been raped and that guards had asked for sexual favours. The findings may lead to a senate inquiry, but surely it should be leading to the release of innocent asylum seekers, not just another investigation.

What I find inexcusable, is that even when inhumane, criminal and degrading behaviour is identified and acknowledged, the government will continue the practices and policies that condone the crimes. I can't help compare the horror stories of Aussie men and women held in prison camps during the Second World War with the horror stories of the men, women and children held on our current watch. When the general population hear historical stories of rape and assault, forced incarceration and beatings in the prison camps we feel disgust and outrage because we identify with the prisoners as our own, our family. People seeking asylum have very deliberately, been kept anonymous to ensure we don't respond with the horror and disgust these current conditions and criminal acts deserve. When I share these stories I deliberately humanise with a name, hoping people will be identifiable as worthy and real to the average Australian.

The *us* and *them* mentality when it comes to people seeking asylum, was highlighted back in 2000 with the fabricated *children overboard* fiasco. The government of the day under Prime Minister John Howard orchestrated the demonisation of the asylum seeker by famously declaring that *we will decide who comes to this country, and the circumstances in which they come.* The propaganda machine kicked into overdrive, with flagrant lies and racist assumptions. The motive was clearly to generate fear and unease among the general population and the ultimate gain was a political win. From this time, the lives of people seeking asylum have been used as political silage to be fed to the masses. The debates rage, views vary and can be polarising but what I hear is the diatribe fed through the Murdoch machine, spewed forth by the contemptuous idiocy of Shock-jock's like Bolt and Jones. I thought that I had heard it all until the Abbott propaganda machine cranked up.

I found the lead into the 2013 election farcical because the political party without a single clear policy won, admittedly there wasn't much of a competition, but to play out an election campaign on the misery of others sickened me. The we will *stop the boats* slogan won Abbott the election with the use of masterful manipulation that the nation greedily swallowed. The *us* versus *them* ideology was warped so significantly that people actually believed stopping the boats was essential to our national survival. It was the overpowering message that people seeking asylum are of lesser value that repulsed me, I kept hearing that asylum seekers don't value their own children's lives. Why else would they risk putting their kids on a boat, they are obviously coming for economic reasons. They can afford to pay thousands of dollars to people smugglers so they must have money and just want to cut corners. They are morally corrupt and definitely can't be trusted. What I heard through all this dialogue was, we are so much better than them, we know how to behave, we would never risk putting our children on a little wooden fishing boat at sea. We know the process and we would be orderly and take our number, wait our turn like the polite people we are because we are far more evolved. There was a complete lack of reality and comprehension of the issues related to seeking asylum in each statement.

Chapter 9

Stop the Boats

The worst sin toward our fellow creatures is not to hate them, but to be indifferent to them; that's the essence of inhumanity.

George Bernard Shaw

The minute the Abbott government was sworn into office, our little team witnessed dramatic change, the Department of Immigration and Citizenship became the Department of Immigration and Border Protection (DIBP). The *Stop the boats* policy kicked in instantly with Operation Sovereign Borders (OSB) led by the defence force and headed by Lieutenant General Angus Campbell. DIBP increased the spin doctors from the usual thirteen to sixty-six and this dynamic team was employed to spread the department message both across the nation and internationally and their work was masterful. What we experienced was a lesson in the power of language, keywords and phrases, such as *'illegal'* were echoed, we were *saving the children from drowning* and *stopping the people smugglers business model.* We heard it repeatedly and people began to use it and pass it on, it was a truly impressive use of propaganda, the message was very loud, clear and regurgitated.

Just when we thought that the demonising was complete, we were provided a greater understanding. We were all told that people seeking asylum are not like us, and we were told that the situation is worse than we initially thought because these people are dangerous. The government were telling us not to worry because we have the expertise of the defence force to protect us from this evil invasion. They will stop the tide of evil, they will turn them back, lock up the ones we already have and send them off to hidden desperate destinations to rot. Don't worry, they will not be let in, we will protect you.

The key campaign enticer used to win votes was the boat issue and part of the *stop the boat* promise was the introduction of a *Regional Deterrence Framework to Combat People Smuggling.* This was budgeted at $420 million, the defence force was to engage with other countries in the region, particularly Indonesia and Sri Lanka, to prevent asylum seekers leaving for Australia. The framework included a $20 million proposal 'The Indonesian community engagement programme' which was to include:

- communications campaigns to raise awareness within local villages that people smuggling is a criminal activity;
- a capped boat buy-back scheme that was to provide an incentive for owners of decrepit and dangerously unsafe boats to sell their boats to government officials rather than people smugglers;
- support for wardens in local communities, whose role was to provide intelligence information to the Indonesian National Police on people smuggling operations;
- the option in exceptional circumstances for bounty payments for the provision of information resulting in significant disruptions or arrests leading to convictions.[26]

The 'buy-the-boats' plan was widely ridiculed, with fact-checking group PolitiFact Australia calling the proposal *ridiculous.* Lieutenant General Campbell told a Senate Estimates committee two months into the OSB program that no boats had been purchased because Indonesia did not support the idea.

DIPB set about their task of moving the goalposts by the 14 December 2013 with new amendments to the Migration Regulations 1994 introduced to *prevent unauthorised arrivals from obtaining permanent protection in Australia.*[27] The government declared that anyone who arrived by boat from 19 July 2013 was never going to settle in Australia, this suddenly meant that there were two cohorts in detention, the pre and post 19 July arrivals. To manage this, the Department of Immigration relocated asylum seekers off Nauru and Manus Island where they had languished for twelve months with no processing and returned them to Christmas Island and mainland detention facilities. Then the transfers of the people who arrived after 19 July started to Nauru.

Pratheesh

On 19 July 2013, two boats arrived, one made the cut off, one didn't, when the department declared a 12pm start time for the new legislation. It seemed harsh to so many people, they complained that the navy had picked them up at sea and held them until the new legislation effected them. We were seeing clients from both cohorts and they were justifiably distressed if they were in the post 19 July group. One such client was Pratheesh, a nineteen-year-old young man from the Batticaloa district of Sri Lanka.

Pratheesh was the youngest of three children and his brother had come to Australia ahead of him and was living in Sydney after being granted a Bridging Visa. His father had worked for twenty years in Qatar as a labourer and his mother and sister were home in Sri Lanka. In 2011 his brother was abducted and beaten by an unknown group of Sinhalese men and they threatened to come after him again so he was forced to flee the country. After his brother fled Pratheesh became the target. He was abducted, tortured and raped by the men, fortunately one of the captors let Pratheesh escape into the jungle so he went into hiding and was eventually forced to flee the country too. His friends and family told him that men continued to look for him, Pratheesh strongly denied any political involvement and said that he didn't know why he and his brother were targeted, apart from their Tamil ethnicity. He had been studying commerce and doing well but when I met him he was struggling to come to terms with the dramatic change of circumstances for himself and his brother. He was also repeatedly told by DIBP that he was never going to step foot on mainland Australia.

On the second session with Pratheesh, he said that it had been a *good week* he was attempting to keep busy with the activities on offer and trying to remain positive. The news amongst the Tamils at the time was that a family have been *screened in*, this made them all jubilant and hopeful, Pratheesh was hopeful that he might be *screened in* too. He had reason to be anxious about returning to Sri Lanka because he had received an update from home that strange men had visited his mother looking for him. The men were unknown to her and claimed to be Pratheesh's friends but his mother knew otherwise and he was sure they were the same men that abducted him.

I took Pratheesh out with two of his friends on a directed outing and we made the most of the time by visiting some beautiful sites on the island. We walked in the jungle, had a picnic and the guys just enjoyed the taste of freedom for a few hours. We laughed and sang and ate together but when I booked Pratheesh for the next session he didn't arrive, he had been deported back to Colombo. He had not been given the opportunity to make a claim for asylum or have a claim assessed and yet he had been detained for ten months. Pratheesh is one of many clients that were returned to Sri Lanka through an agreement between our government and the Sinhalese governed Sri Lanka. There is no such arrangement with Iraq, Iran, Somalia, Burma or Sudan and so the Tamils are once again political fodder.

Another consequence of the change in government really disturbed me. When the Department of Immigration and Citizenship changed to the Department of Immigration and Border Protection (DIBP) the care factor among Immigration staff changed with it. In the past clients had developed a relationship with their immigration case manager, some case managers had worked really hard for their clients and they had pushed for small changes in accommodation, access to medical needs, additional activities and to speed up access to the immigration review board. In fact, during my first couple of years on the island, Thursday was the day people would be flown to Perth as free citizens after receiving their permanent visa. Those Thursdays were wonderful, if we had a bad day at the office, you could be guaranteed a feel-good moment if you headed to the little airport. People were often detained for a year or eighteen months at a time after their Refugee Status Assessment had been rejected and then they were finally granted a permanent humanitarian visa following a review process. By this time, they had often established a great rapport with their immigration case manager, who would sometimes be found at the airport waving them off. This all changed dramatically when the Gillard government reintroduced RPCs, there was no longer a requirement for the case management model because asylum claims were not being processed. The case managers continued to exist but in a role of messenger rather than processor, with their caseloads increased due to the change in job description they remained accessible to the clients but started to lose a personal connection.

The DIBP case management team rather abruptly evolved into a new breed, I witnessed good kind people become closed off and cold. They were directed to be purely task driven and they had bought into the *saving the nation from an evil threat* propaganda. There was a high element of fear driving this change because DIBP turned their spin doctors back on their own. When the office of the Prime Minister released a memo stating that employees would be found to be in breach of the code of conduct if they emailed derogatory material about the prime minister, it was laughable. However, for people working in a government system where emails can be checked and breaches will be acted on, no one wanted to be made a scapegoat. The new government had introduced a totalitarian regime overnight and immigration staff reacted to this in a very negative way.

One man comes to mind very clearly, he was once a person that I could rely on for his empathy and compassion. If I needed help from immigration case management on a client's behalf he was a case manager I would contact. We occasionally socialised together as he had a great sense of humour, enjoyed a laugh, but was also interesting and interested. Under DIBP management I witnessed his personality change, he cut himself off and became too busy, too important and accepted a position at a higher level. He became very officious and completely removed from the misery of the clients and the impact this was having on them. I observed that he became the new norm, the standard DIBP worker, if immigration staff couldn't agree with the policy and the abhorrent practices then they were out. I watched as good people left and others adapted to the party line, the lack of processing and case management meant that immigration staff didn't truly get to know any of the people they detained. They were sent to the island to work at the IDC but they were very evidently working to promote the policies of the Department of Immigration and not for the people seeking asylum and it is easier to deliver bad policy when compassion is removed.

The new department came with immense secrecy and a message that we the nation were being protected from a surge of evil, *the illegals*. The previous government had allowed all record of boat arrivals available to the public but with *Operation Sovereign Borders* in full swing, boats were being turned back, people forced into orange rescue pods at sea and turned back toward Indonesia, and the public were not privy to the information. The Minister for Immigration, Scott Morrison was adamant he would limit any information provided to a weekly media briefing with Lieutenant General Campbell and there would be no further information released. This caused a lot of angst when both men would consistently refuse to answer questions citing *operational reasons.*

In the media we were hearing the same old rhetoric, *there have been no boats since the new government came to power* however on Christmas Island we could see a boat off the shore the very day another one of these official statements was released, the boat was held back by the navy and forced back out to sea. The weekly briefings stopped in December 2014, after only two months and evolved into the minister issuing written statements until he refused to release any information at all. Prime Minister Abbott defended the Coalition's approach to releasing information about asylum seeker boats, likening Operation Sovereign Borders to being at war, *if we were at war we wouldn't be giving out information that is of use to the enemy just because we might have an idle curiosity about it ourselves.* The new order was well and truly upon us and the impact was a complete demonisation of people seeking asylum, with the new language repeated with the intent to vilify. The clients were no longer to be referred to as clients they were *detainees* and when they were transferred to Nauru or to Manus Island they were labelled *transferees.* Minister Scott Morrison's instructions included directing staff to replace the term *asylum seeker* with *illegal maritime arrival,* this change in the language was another deliberate attempt to further dehumanise. Our service refused to use this language and were forced to witness all other agencies accept the changes. The CPPM became the DPPM, our service was the only one using the word, *client* and once again we were fighting to provide dignity to people who became victims of political spin.

Families in detention

The very obvious problem with holding families in detention for long periods of time is the inability for a family unit to function. Relationships are tested to the maximum just in fleeing a country, let alone taking a dangerous journey to safety. The expectation is that on arrival the family will have time to breathe, to take stock of what has happened to them and to then start to function again, but this is where it starts to unravel. At a guess I would say the majority of people that arrived on Christmas Island during my five years were from very low to middle-class, no matter the ethnic background, generally the male was the breadwinner and the female was the stay-at-home Mum. The traditional roles meant the wife had the babies and would tend the house and cook, the husband would provide, detention centres don't cater for this. There are no cooking facilities, there is no useful task for men, there is no home to clean, women grieve the ability to nurture and people lose their sense of place in the world. This is okay if you're detained for three months or so, people can put up with it but, when the detainment is ongoing indefinitely for a year, or two, or more, it's damaging. The living conditions in Construction Camp (CC) were primitive at their best because this was originally a temporary construction workers' camp with old transportable buildings known as *dongers* joined together with covered walkways. The *dongers* are tiny, some had been joined together to create two rooms and some of them had a small bathroom added, but the majority of people used communal bathrooms, the floor space is about two metre square and this was the only private space allocated to a family. In this space babies were expected to learn to crawl and walk and share the area with parents and older siblings. It's not an environment suitable for a baby to meet the normal developmental milestones and so to put it simply, they don't.

In the grounds there is very limited space to play, one basketball court and a small playground only added in recent years. The Christmas Island Cricket and Sporting Club is located in front of CC and when I first arrived the Department of Immigration had established an agreement that families and UAMs could access the oval twice daily, under escort with Serco guards and obviously only available when it wasn't raining or there wasn't a staff shortage. Serco seemed to always be short staffed and it's a tropical island where it rains a lot, so of course there were countless occasions when the walk across to the oval didn't happen. But even this small window of opportunity was removed for months at a time when members of the community and members of the club made repeated complaints to Serco and immigration that the asylum seekers or *Reffo's* as many people called them, were not respecting the grounds by repeatedly littering the oval. The complaints were warranted, but how simple is it to educate and lead by example, Serco staff were reluctant to do that, so the complaints were once again dealt with in a punitive manner. The privilege of a stroll on the oval or a kick of a ball was removed, with very limited activity and restricted opportunity to have any time on their own, or as a family unit, relationships suffered. Parenting became a problem and the ability to function well as a parent in such an environment was constantly tested.

When I wandered into CC, Serco staff would often complain that people weren't watching their children, *they were just letting them run wild.* Eventually Serco created a position for a family liaison worker and a toy library was set up for the families where parents were encouraged to play and interact with their kids as much as possible and it had a positive impact. It was great while it lasted but unfortunately the workers left and the position was never replaced, I was asking for weeks, which eventually rolled into months when the replacement was coming. At one-point Serco informed everyone at the CPPM that a replacement was being sent from the family detention centre outside Adelaide called Inverbrackie then we found out that she was being used in another position. When I enquired with the Serco manager he told me it was absolutely none of my business and of course the position was never filled because it wasn't in the contract and Serco would not be fined for not filling the position. For sole parents the harsh conditions of detainment were heightened because they had little support and there was no one to leave the children with, they were unable to access classes and activities. Even going for a shower or to the toilet was made hard because they would often be made to queue with a hungry or sleeping child. There were constant requests for access to some type of child care to help the parent but these were ignored.

Anyone who is a parent will identify with the strong innate protective factor that sets in when you have a child and people seeking asylum are strong evidence of this. They have made the greatest sacrifice and the hardest choice trying to save their kids by bringing them on the boat. A parent only puts their child on a boat when there is no alternative, if you are reading this as a parent, can you honestly say that you wouldn't do anything to try to protect your child, love is love after all. It is no different if a person is from Baghdad, Tehran, Kabul, Jaffna, Sydney, Canberra or Bendigo parental love and protection is the same. Additionally, the same can be said when a child's needs aren't being met, parents will ask for help and when this is ignored, they demand; when this is ignored they protest and this was the pattern in each compound. People were *managed* in a punitive manner and genuine concerns were not addressed because detention centres are reactive environments and preventative help is very rarely considered.

Another compounding issue for families in detention, is the enormous power advantage an immigration or Serco worker has over an asylum seeker. From the moment a person stepped onto the jetty at Flying Fish Cove they became powerless. Seeking asylum means handing over any freedom of choice and any ability to determine your own destiny and this becomes evident immediately. People are fed what's on the menu; they are told when to eat it; where to sleep; and that if they don't like it *they can just go back home.* I certainly had many clients complain to me of Serco and in one incident an immigration case manager telling people to *just go home if you don't like it.* That powerlessness doesn't take long to develop into resentment, then into mistrust, followed by hopelessness. When even the simplest of decisions are taken from a person, it's harder to identify yourself, for not only is your culture and custom gone, but a confidence in who you are is missing. This is when people find themselves thanking immigration, IHMS and Serco for providing something that is just a basic right. For example, when families were split up across compounds there was a major power shift, Serco and immigration would sanction the authority for a family to visit one another, but it was conditional and people had to show gratitude and display worthiness.

Immigration and Serco staff believed that all people should conform to the rules and regulations imposed, even when a child was suffering. The *us* and *them* mentality kicked in loud and clear, there is no room for flexibility with this style of management. Some Serco officers thought that if they gave someone extra attention it would encourage *bad behaviour*, it never ceased to amaze me that Serco staff expected all these poor people to conform and to show appreciation. I witnessed countless occasions when people were ridiculed and belittled, many of the Serco officers were ex-prison guards and brought their prison gaoler attitudes with them. They treated people as criminals and gradually those detained assumed their new identity; the prisoner, shamed, belittled and intimidated.

Some of the concerns I had with the treatment of families was with the provision of basic medical needs. In 2013 and 2014 there was a waiting list of forty-four people waiting for replacement eyeglasses. Many were children who had lost their glasses on the journey, they waited over six months for an optometrist to be flown to the island for eye tests and another four months until they received their glasses. I was seeing a sixteen-year-old girl who struggled with very impaired vision for ten months, she desperately needed glasses after losing them on the boat, when she finally received them, she felt obliged to express appreciation for the enormous sacrifice immigration had made on her behalf. There was no recognition from immigration that ten months with severely impaired vision was distressing and that the anguish could easily have been alleviated months earlier. The Health Liaison Officer attributed the delay to *scheduling problems* it seemed that getting an optometrist booked and flown on to the island was a major feat.

Rashid

Families often arrived with a multitude of medical or psychological problems brought about by the persecution they had been forced to flee. Eleven-year-old Rashid was one of the children I worked with who came under this category. Rashid's parents travelled from Iran with their two young sons, his Persian father had married an Iranian Arab and this was a frowned upon *love marriage* with the people in their community not accepting it. They waited until Rashid was nine years old and then made their move, Rashid was abducted and repeatedly raped as retribution to the family for their mixed marriage. When he was released home, he confided in his father that he wanted to kill himself, he was extremely traumatised and his behaviour reverted to that of a six-year-old. His parents took him to three psychologists and eventually on a pilgrimage to the Imam Reza Holy Shrine in Mashhad but nothing seemed to work. The family was in turmoil and then they received a threat that their youngest son was to be the next victim, so they did not hesitate in planning an escape. They knew that relocating within Iran was not an option because the same misery would pursue them, so they fled the country. Rashid's maternal uncle joined them on the journey however, he was sent to NWP on arrival and was not allowed to stay with the family.

I received Rashid's referral from an IHMS psychologist, she had worked with Rashid but was struggling to build rapport and was very anxious that the family may end up on a transfer list to Manus Island or Nauru, she wanted input from my team. Rashid was presenting with some psychotic features attributed to immense trauma, he was experiencing auditory hallucinations, hearing a voice say *'come'* he was also experiencing horrific nightmares that made him too frightened to sleep without the light on. He was very withdrawn, rarely left his father's side and he was in a constant heightened state of arousal, in other words, he was scared stiff. The poor kid felt enormous guilt and shame, and struggled with this negative emotional state, he was hyper vigilant and would startle very easily and to add to his misery not long after he was detained on Christmas Island, he started wetting the bed. Rashid told me that he was missing his uncle and was worried about him being alone with all the strange men at NWP.

Whenever I worked with a child so evidently traumatised the very first thing I did was add him or her to the CPPM agenda for discussion because children should not be detained in an environment that promotes fear and mistrust. I started working with Rashid and his father on addressing some of the immediate needs, such as focussing on ways to reduce his level of anxiety. I was able to build rapport with them because of my experience living in Iran, by chatting about the famous sights we had seen and the countryside. I was acutely aware that I would not be able to speak to Rashid without his father until he fully trusted me and so we had many sessions when we simply drank tea and talked about Iran. I made sure that his uncle was added to the list to attend our service to enable the whole family time together on the veranda and I took them out on directed outings. Unfortunately, Rashid and his family had arrived after the reintroduction of regional processing they were told that they would be going to either Manus Island or Nauru but, at the CPPM I petitioned for a mainland solution. Rashid desperately needed to be in an environment where he felt safe. He certainly didn't have a sense of safety in Aqua compound, he also needed access to good quality psychiatric care that would treat his emerging psychosis and prevent further deterioration in his mental state. Rashid was a very sick child and although IHMS and our service were appealing to immigration to have him transferred to the mainland, it took months. He eventually became so unwell that he and his father were added to a list on a charter flight to Darwin where they were detained in a Darwin IDC for two months. The family had been separated with his beloved uncle in NWP, his mother and brother in Aqua compound and Rashid and his father in Darwin. He became so distressed that he threatened suicide and was taken to hospital for a psychiatric admission. The psychiatrist advised that Rashid should be reunited with his family and released from the detention environment and he was discharged the next day and sent to a detention centre in Inverbrackie in South Australia. He was reunited with his mother and brother however, his uncle was left on Christmas Island.

After they had spent two and a half months in Inverbrackie I received a referral from IHMS, the family had been returned to Christmas Island and Rashid was very unwell. I scheduled the first available appointment and Rashid sat with me and told me that he was very sad to have been returned to the island, because in Inverbrackie he spent every day at school and was able to go to the swimming pool in the afternoons. His days were filled and he made friends and was *not worried all the time.* His father told me that Rashid had stopped bed wetting and only had infrequent nightmares but since their return to Christmas Island there had been a noticeable deterioration in his mood. He had started wetting the bed again and was experiencing nightmares causing insomnia, because he was too afraid to sleep. His father raised new concerns; his son had become irritable and quick to anger, something uncharacteristic and new since arriving back on the island. Rashid was scared, he had lost all sense of safety and wanted to stay close to his parents at all times and his hyper-vigilance had resurfaced.

What I found suspiciously unusual was the fact that I only needed to discuss Rashid once at the CPPM before the family were added to a transfer list, they were returned to Inverbrackie within the month. Rumours circulated that the family had been transferred back to Christmas Island against the psychiatrist's advice and that the psychiatrist was threatening to go public. Another rumour was that they had been returned to the island in error and the Department of Immigration was desperately trying to fix it before the *shit hit the fan,* the rumours were disturbing because we all knew that transferring a whole family in error was most likely true. The one positive outcome was that I was able to put a fast-track request through to the torture and trauma counselling service that visited Inverbrackie, this ensured Rashid would access consistent care for his trauma symptoms and I was able to provide a clinical handover. Poor Rashid, he and his family really suffered unnecessarily due to a public servants error.

Another cohort of people seeking asylum that are incredibly vulnerable are pregnant women and newborn babies, they should not be in a detention centre and certainly not in a remote location. Christmas Island does not have the facility to deliver, monitor and maintain the life of premature babies, nor does the local health service have a resident obstetrician or paediatrician to provide regular consultation and monitoring of difficult pregnancies and sick babies. The flight time direct to Perth is four hours, therefore a medical evacuation (Medi-vac) off the island will take a minimum of eight hours to allow a plane to come to the island and turn around and go back. Obviously the reality is that a medivac may take ten, fifteen, twenty hours or more, because a plane has to be made available and the appropriate arrangements have to be made. The other huge logistical factor is that not only are planes not always available, they are also not always able to land on the island due to the fluctuating weather conditions which wreak havoc at the airstrip. The island airstrip is covered with clouds of condensation after rain, this makes it impossible for pilots to land, planes are limited in the amount of time spent circling waiting for a break in the clouds, because they may have to turn around and fly back without landing.

The babies born on the mainland and returned to Christmas Island all had mothers that were completely distraught by July 2014. They had accessed lawyers through the law firm Maurice Blackburn and the lawyers had made a visit to the families and were trying to get their case through to the High Court of Australia. The dialogue between the Department of Immigration and the lawyers representing the women and babies was hampered by lengthy delays for requested information and what appeared to be deliberately obstructive behaviour. The women were at constant threat of being transferred to Nauru and became highly anxious, so they decided to conduct a peaceful protest within CC, but this escalated when it was badly handled by Serco staff. The women came to the decision that if they were to leave their newborn babies with Serco in the canteen area and walk away as a sign of disgust it would send a strong message of their level of distress. Unfortunately, the Serco officers escalated the scene into one of chaos by using their usual form of correctional management that is, to threaten and intimidate. Some of the women became so distressed they self-harmed, with one woman climbing up a building and throwing herself off the roof, there were no severe physical injuries but the psychological damage was done. These events were preventable and more importantly the whole disgraceful scene was witnessed by the children in the compound, the women felt helpless and now hopeless, it was yet another blow to their already fragile mental states. The response from IHMS was to offer more medication to sedate the problem and from Immigration and Serco it was punitive action.

Negative security assessments

For the first three years of my work on Christmas Island the processing of asylum claims took place on the island. Refugee Status Assessments (RSAs) were conducted by immigration staff and if a person was found to meet the criteria as a refugee they would go through a security clearance prior to be granted a Protection Visa. The security assessment was conducted by the Australian Security Intelligence Organisation (ASIO) and if they handed down an adverse assessment, the person was kept in detention indefinitely. The person would receive this news from Immigration and would not be given any detail of the assessment, just told that they had failed the security assessment and would not be offered a protection visa in Australia. ASIO did not have to explain themselves or their findings, they simply made a blanket decision yes, you're in, or no, you're not, the assessment was final. There was no appeal or review process available and people were told that although they were recognised as a refugee, they were not welcome to stay in Australia. Under our international non-refoulement obligations we could not return these people to their country of origin as it was deemed too unsafe, we had recognised they were at risk of persecution. The only options available were to wait until the country of origin is safer and the circumstances allow a return or find a third country willing to accept the person.

Pramada

Between January 2010 and November 2011, ASIO had issued fifty-four adverse security assessments to offshore entry persons, out of seven thousand cases considered. In contrast, not a single adverse assessment was issued to an 'onshore' refugee between mid-2008 and mid-2011.[28] For one family I met, the impact of a negative security assessment was just horrendous. I received a referral for Pramada a thirty-five-year-old Tamil woman who was experiencing multiple symptoms of traumatic stress.

Pramada was short and round with gorgeous dark curly hair and eyes that I only witnessed as puffy from an endless stream of tears. I could see that under very different circumstances she would be fun and lively but when I met her she was sad and depleted. She had been born and raised in Jaffna to a family of six children, but in 1993 while she was studying her final high school certificate her father was killed during conflict. Her family went through periods of displacement over the years when the fighting intensified but somehow Pramada managed to study a degree in economics and became an accountant. Pramada married and had two children, when we met her daughter was six-years-old, her son was two and she was about twelve weeks pregnant.

During the last couple of years of the civil war Pramada was approached at her workplace by a representative of the LTTE, he told her they needed a new accountant to manage the organisations funds and Pramada was chosen. She was not happy about this because she knew that working in any capacity with the LTTE would make her and her family a potential target but she was not given a choice, this was a directive. So Pramada did the books for a recognised terrorist organisation and this was to be her downfall.

Immediately after the end of the civil war in 2009 her husband and one of her brothers left Sri Lanka and arrived by boat on Christmas Island. Pramada, her children, another brother and her mother followed on another boat and were rescued by the Australian customs vessel *Oceanic Viking.*

The seventy-eight Sri Lankans on board refused to leave the vessel after it took them to Bintan Indonesia and a political standoff took place until an agreement was made that all on board would be processed for entry into Australia within four weeks.

Pramada was reunited with her husband and brother on Christmas Island and their Refugee Status assessments were conducted but the outcome was not good for Pramada. Although they were all recognised as refugees, she failed the security assessment. Her mother and brothers were granted protection visas and sent to the mainland. However Pramada was told that she could not be offered protection in Australia, she was told they would be detained until Australia found another country to send them to. The word soon spread among the Tamil population in detention and Pramada felt unjustly discriminated against on a daily basis. She knew that she was the subject of gossip among the others in detention and she gradually withdrew, hardly wanting to leave her small room. Her health was affected as she was pregnant and suffering with terrible morning sickness and the negative comments were felt even harder.

Trying to provide effective trauma-focussed counselling was difficult with Pramada because she had enormous worries and guilt. She felt completely helpless and also responsible for the situation her family where in. She had wanted to be honest during her refugee assessment and had assumed that in disclosing her forced work with the LTTE she would be exempt from any true affiliation with the group as she was not a willing participant.

On one occasion Pramada presented in distress as her husband had been informed by their lawyer that there had not been an application made on their behalf to the UNHCR for placement in another country. She was adamant that Immigration had told her this had been done months prior. She felt that they are being used as a political example to warn others, that they had been victimised and exploited, and the strain was having a damaging psychological impact on each member of her family. Pramada started to experience insomnia and nausea, the combination made her easily frustrated and short tempered with the children and the children were heavily dependent on her presence. She complained that she couldn't even go to the toilet without taking one of the kids with her. They were traumatised children, her young son was in the habit of laying on the floor when he heard a plane fly overhead as he waited for a bomb to drop. When she watched this behaviour she felt even more parental guilt for the trauma her children had been exposed to.

We talked about her own exposure to the horrors of war and the symptoms she was dealing with. Pramada would sometimes wake in fright from the loud sound made by the air conditioning unit outside her room because it reminded her of the sound of jet fighters coming in close overhead in the conflict. Waking in fear triggered her traumatic memories, one recurring memory was of the death of a nine-month-old child during heavy shelling. Pramada watched as the baby girl's lower face was blown away, she said that the baby stared at her in shock and she found it hard to get the image of this baby girl out of her mind. Pramada described numerous events that she has experienced during the conflict and they were recalled with clarity causing her immense distress. She would often present for a session in a depressed and teary state and felt that it was incredibly unjust to give her a negative assessment without the capacity to appeal the decision. She wanted to know exactly what had been said about her, but the only information provided was that she not to be granted a protection visa for security reasons and her repeated requests for a reason failed.

Her lawyers also complained that there was no information made available to them. Her lawyer had been appointed by the Australian Tamil Congress and had waited months to receive any feedback on his request for her immigration file. When the feedback finally came, it was that the person working on the case was on leave, so he needed to wait. One day Pramada told me that she had been unexpectedly interviewed again by ASIO, for nearly four hours and the interview really upset her. She said they kept repeating the same questions and she kept replying but she also took the opportunity to focus on the indignation and sense of shame she felt as a result of being accused of having a terrorist link. She demanded the ASIO officers supply an apology for her loss of reputation among the Tamil community and she became upset when they refused to comply.

The months were ticking by and Pramada was due to be flown off the island for the delivery of her baby, on Christmas Island pregnant women are flown off at no later than thirty-four weeks to prevent delivery on the island, which meant the next battle had arrived. The Department of Immigration was seriously considering separating Pramada from her husband and children while she flew off to have the baby, I added her to the CPPM agenda so I could advocate keeping the family together. I expressed her concerns over the possibility that she may be separated from her husband and children and the negative impact this forced separation would have on each of them and of course I found it frustrating that I should need to spell this out. Pramada's fear and anxiety were escalating, she was having even more difficulty sleeping, eating and concentrating and she was heavily pregnant. Immigration eventually allowed the family to stay together and they were transferred to the mainland where they were housed within a detention centre where they were allowed visits from her mother and brothers. Pramada delivered a healthy baby, but this little one was destined to be detained indefinitely. Her daughter was enrolled in a public school and this was great for them because they could introduce some form of normality into the little girl's world, until a newspaper journalist outed the family. Pramada phoned me one day in distress, a newspaper report had declared that Australian taxpayers were funding the education of the child of a terrorist. Pramada was frightened for her children's safety and her daughter had to be withdrawn from the school.

By May 2012 there were fifty people detained indefinitely in the Australian detention system, but the complaints started to be heard. A legal challenge made its way into the High Court of Australia and in October

2012 the High Court ruled that an asylum seeker deemed by ASIO to be a security risk can still be granted a protection visa. In a case brought by lawyer David Manne on behalf of a Sri Lankan asylum seeker, a majority of the High Court held that a decision to refuse the asylum seeker a protection visa after he received an adverse security assessment by ASIO had not been made according to law, and that a regulation which prevented the granting of the protection visa was invalid. The government relented and introduced a review process. Margaret Stone a retired federal court judge was appointed the first independent reviewer, with the ability to access all the material ASIO had used to decide someone is a threat, asylum seekers with a negative assessment were granted the right to have negative assessments reviewed every twelve months. This review process is not written into legislation and is in itself at risk of a reversal and the process continues to be a breach of human rights.

Pramada's case was one of the first to be reviewed and she had her negative security decision successfully reversed, with no explanation or detail provided. After four years of detainment she was finally granted protection and was able to live freely in the community but by this time her trauma symptoms had intensified and become chronic. Since 2013 twenty people have had their decisions reversed and have been granted protection visas. The reasons for the reversals have not been made public and the remaining thirty people continue to be told nothing. In March 2015 the United Nations Human Rights Committee released a damning report on Australia's *cruel and degrading* practice of locking up refugees indefinitely on the basis of secret ASIO assessments without a right of appeal, Prime Minister Abbott's response was that *Australians are sick of being lectured to by the United Nations.*

Chapter 10

This Is Happiness

A child without education is like a bird without wings.

Tibetan proverb

In 2007 the Christmas Island District High School (CIDHS) received additional funding through the Department of Immigration to provide education to asylum seeker children. The school was funded to financially cover the additional costs of employment of teaching staff and for additional resources and for CIDHS the agreement proved to be quite lucrative. The kids were taken out from detention and transported by bus to the school each day but they were taught in separate classrooms to the island kids due to their varied skills base. For many kids it was their first introduction to school, they were all taught in English and the timetable consisted of English language, Australia studies, art and craft and physical education, they were not offered a mainstream curriculum in line with the Western Australian Department of Education. Following some complaints from the island residents about the questionable age of male UAMs attending the local school it was decided that the older children would be taught in school rooms brought in to the Phosphate Hill site, opposite CC.

I got to know some of the teachers in my first three years, they were enthusiastic, passionate about their work and loved the kids. Occasionally parents were brought out of detention to attend a few special school assemblies and events like Harmony Day and the sports carnival. It was always a great atmosphere with so many nationalities mixing together, but these were the only times that the kids and families had the opportunity to mingle. Unfortunately the quantity and quality of the education gradually deteriorated, with no apparent answerability on how the immigration funding was managed or mismanaged. The teaching staff changed and the level of expertise and enthusiasm drastically diminished and by 2013 children were receiving just 1.5 hours of schooling each day which included a short break scheduled for the teaching staff. Due to the large number of kids in detention they alternated attendance between two groups, one week on, and one week off, so children didn't bother attending. I was often told by UAMs that it was a complete waste of time and all they did was craft and a bit of sport. The lack of education was a massive concern for the parents, understandably they wanted their children to learn and develop and what they saw worried them. Our team heard this complaint repeatedly from our clients, the kids were missing out on the opportunity to be educated, and they were bored and withdrawn. Parents complained and as was commonplace with any parental complaint nothing was done about it until the Human Rights Commission visited.

In March 2014 representatives from the Australian Human Rights Team visited the island to conduct interviews with each family and UAM. They were conducting a National Inquiry into Children in Immigration Detention, prompted by increasing reports of self-harm by mothers with young children. In a desperate attempt to cover up the squalor, the family camp received new paint, new plants and a thorough clean with a high-pressure hose so we knew someone important was coming. When Gillian Trigg, Australia's Human Rights Commissioner arrived she announced that she would be available for a public meeting at the community recreation centre and encouraged anyone with any interest in children in detention to attend. There were only about twenty-five people that turned up and not a single representative from CIDHS bothered to come along. I raised the concern that the current level of education on offer was woefully inadequate and that it was a cause of great angst to parents and older children who knew they were falling far behind.

When the initial findings of the investigation into children in detention was released education was highlighted as a concern raised by most parents and UAMs. With the spotlight on Christmas Island, the CIDHS finally lost the funding and a new Christmas Island Learning Centre was created by the Catholic Education Department WA. There were nineteen full time positions advertised for teaching staff and well over one hundred teachers applied. At long last the children received the level of education they had craved, and the kids, families and teachers were delighted. It was such a pity that it was brought about by such dire circumstance and after hundreds of children had missed out.

By this time the Aqua and Lilac sites were empty as many families had been transferred to Nauru. The Department of Immigration relocated the transportable buildings from these sites into the Phosphate Hill site opposite CC and a school was created within two weeks. This included new school uniforms, signage, a school crossing, volumes of educational resources and volunteer escort jobs for parents or young adults in the family camp. The school principal was enthusiastic and a breath of fresh air, it wasn't all smooth sailing though, he was an educator who was obviously very skilled and highly regarded by his team, but he had never been exposed to the madness of immigration bureaucracy. One of the most abhorrent practices they were confronted with was the immigration and Serco staff referring to the children by boat number. The school refused to comply, thank God and truly offered a caring and dignified education. This amazing team of educators were the cream of the crop, despite being dictated to in a condescending manner by public servants and they worked hard and received little acknowledgment for it.

Our team were excited to meet the teachers because we all had children on our caseloads so we met with the teaching staff and delivered an information session on our service and the common symptoms we saw in a traumatised child. We offered to liaise with individual teachers and families when a child's behaviours attributed to trauma may need addressing. This offer was utilised on a few occasions until the school received a directive from the Department of Immigration that they were not to enter into any discussions with our service due to the Privacy Policy and client confidentiality. We also received the same directive, my argument that discussion was in the interest of the child and with full consent of the parents was to no avail. This highlighted to me at the time just how secretive and extremely guarded the Department of Immigration had become, they were anxious we would disclose the lack of care and humanity that was clearly evident and our service was being viewed as a liability. The fact that the Department of Immigration regarded our little team as a threat was not missed by my colleagues and me, because we were being cut out of access to dialogue regarding our clients and also to the very limited access points to provide input into client care.

The school closed in December 2014 after functioning for only six months. This followed the passing of the changes to the Migration and Maritime Powers Legislation Amendment Bill. The debate over holding children in indefinite detention caused great angst in the senate and a deal with the then Minister for Immigration Scott Morrison. He negotiated his dodgy changes on the proviso that children should be removed from immigration detention on Christmas Island by Christmas 2014 and true to his word the last of the families were sent off the island but they were simply detained elsewhere. He didn't promise they would be released from other immigration detention centres in the network.

Christmas Island Community

Christmas Island is remote, it's located in the Indian Ocean approximately 380 km south of Java Head Indonesia and approximately 2,650 km from Perth. The Island has an area of 135 square kilometres and a multi-cultural population of predominantly Chinese, Malay and European background. When I first arrived on Christmas Island I expected to find a highly informed population among the locals because the immigration policy, the plight of asylum seekers and refugees has a direct impact on this tiny community of just less than 2,000 and yet there was an almost total disconnect. Some of the whingeing that I heard in the community was startling. Unreasonable tales circulated and grew with each telling which included accusations that people detained were making irrational demands for fresh fruit and vegetables to be flown on to the island and that people were complaining about not getting access to cosmetic surgery.

A popular misconception is that asylum seekers are poverty stricken and fleeing with just the clothes on their backs and this image also caused problems. Not all people who seek asylum are without funds because wealth does not offer total protection from persecution. Many Iranians and Iraqis flee due to political or religious persecution, they may have lived a wealthy lifestyle but are unable to leave their country legitimately, they are just as persecuted as the poor Afghan villager. When these people arrive with money or designer clothes they have been labelled *economic refugees* and some local residents made a point of taking photos of the people arriving by boat, to sell their photos to the press and would be the first to vilify anyone seen with any semblance of wealth. Ironically these same people failed to recognise their own abhorrent behaviour by taking advantage of vulnerable people for financial gain. They were intent on demonising, spreading untruths and remaining ignorant to help polarise the views on the island.

This very beautiful little island has a permanent population that could and should be the most informed in Australia. In the five years I lived there we received over 900 boats that either sailed right up to the jetty or were located further out at sea and people were brought into shore on navy or customs ship. Either way the island community witnessed bedraggled, frightened and exhausted men, women and children arrive by the thousand and yet a large population of Christmas Island chose to disengage. From my understanding, before I arrived, when there were a few boats that trickled over from Indonesia, the community was very welcoming and hands-on; they fed people themselves from their own pantry cupboards, which is generous considering the high cost of living and the sporadic arrival of supplies. This generosity of spirit changed over a relatively short time. With the increase of boat arrivals people decided that it was too hard to remain engaged, locals would talk about the days when they helped the *Reffos* and I would be left feeling confused. Was there a cut-off point to generosity and compassion that I was oblivious to? If you help out a few times does that mean you don't need too anymore? Are people granted a pardon from caring because they once did something good?

When I first arrived on Christmas Island there were still people being housed in community detention on the island, several families and a few single Tamil men. From the stories I was told by the locals, people really enjoyed getting to know them and welcoming them into their homes and into their lives. Unfortunately due to a housing shortage, the houses had to be handed over to immigration workers and by the middle of 2010 there was no community detention on the island. It was a real shame to lose because there was no longer a connection between the community and people seeking asylum and the detention centre emphasised the harsh difference between *us* and *them*.

The common reference to the North West Point detention centre as *the dark side* was very disturbing, people complained about having the detention centre there and yet they reaped the benefits from it. There were local businesses bringing in huge profits just in food and basic grocery supplies, while others rented out housing and vehicles and made a small fortune. There were jobs galore and most families were on two incomes with cleaning and maintenance jobs paying very well. The economic benefit was substantial however, there was little cultural benefit with people remaining disinterested and ignorant, when they could have been involved and informed. There were still a small handful of residents who truly did care known as *the Reffo lovers,* but they were very much a minority on the island. They would donate toys and clothes, they volunteered their time, helped at events and wanted to support, their kindness helped sustain me.

Island services

Anyone who's ever lived in a very remote location will have some understanding of the problems associated with remote living. Some of the issues are merely tiresome, for example the cost of getting to the island is exorbitant and made visits from friends and family prohibitive, when they could easily have a European holiday for the same price. The fruit and vegetables are flown onto the island at astronomical costs, a regular iceberg lettuce can cost $15 or more and a punnet of strawberries would be $10.50. I remember buying a small slice of watermelon for Bella for $9 and I once paid $36 for a packet of sausages for a barbeque because I was in a hurry and didn't check the price and they certainly weren't gourmet. The mail was delivered once a week and when I first arrived it was flown to Kuala Lumpur in Malaysia and then flown over on a weekly Malaysian Airlines flight. Now it arrives on the Virgin Airways flight from Perth and any parcels that are not posted in an Express postage bag end up coming on the cargo ship with all the dry goods. For many years it was the *Princess Mary*, now it's the *ASCL Michele* that sails from Fremantle and makes her way to Christmas and the Cocos (Keeling) Islands and on to Singapore and back. It was not unusual for rough sea conditions to prevent the ship from coming in for months. Supplies would become very low on the shelves and some of the biggest topics of conversation were: *how's the swell* and *when's the ship coming in?* It wasn't only mail and supplies that could be a problem, so too was working and living in a very small community. The cost of healthy food is high but there is no goods and services tax (GST) applied to cigarettes and alcohol. A packet of cigarettes when I first arrived was $3 and a large bottle of Bombay

Sapphire gin $17 needless to say I enjoyed a gin and tonic at the end of most days with tonic water the costly part that I had to stock up on when the ship came in.

With every remote community there are people who drift in who are running from some heartache or misery and for some crazy reason think that a remote location with cheap booze and very limited resources is the key to happiness. The problem is there are very limited services available on Christmas Island to support these people. Several years ago the Department of Regional Australia Territories office which is the governing body signed a service delivery agreement with Western Australia Child Protection. Child protection would second a senior social worker to cover both Christmas and Cocos Islands. The role was designed to provide support to the permanent population with assistance to the aged, people with disabilities, financial concerns and relationship issues. With a population of 2,000 on Christmas Island and 650 people on Cocos, the one social worker was often inadequate and not necessarily skilled in the areas that mattered, such as drug and alcohol, disability and aged care. Why the arrangement was made with a child protection social worker is unclear because there is very little need for child protection work in both communities and it is actually the AFP on the islands that are the legal representatives due to the commonwealth governance, not WA Child Protection.

Anyone with a mental illness was managed by the GP, this led to the health service signing an agreement with the WA education department to utilise the school psychologist a few hours a week for the community to access. This arrangement was terminated in 2013 due to a poor uptake and lack of community engagement, most people simply didn't know about the arrangement. When the boat arrivals increased and with that, the fly-in-fly-out population of Serco, IHMS, Immigration and AFP staff, we started picking up the slack. Our service was based at the local health service, so it was an unwritten agreement that we would see members of the community who may present for a variety of reasons, a severe mental illness, grief reaction, depression or anxiety disorder. To manage it, we preferred a referral from the GP, we couldn't advertise or promote our service because we were fully funded by Immigration for asylum seekers only. There were only four of us and we always had a small list of community clients on our books, plus a waitlist of over 100 for T&T counselling so to manage it we would often see the community clients after hours. The other work we did was to support the community in times of crisis, suicides, deaths at sea, traumatic events and to provide crisis assessments.

Christmas Island is similar to many small communities, its run by volunteers, there is the Volunteer Marine Rescue, the Fire Brigade, the Saint John's Ambulance Service, CI Charities, they run the very busy kiosk at the airport and the opportunity shop, the toy library, environmental action groups and the Christmas Island outdoor cinema club. In addition, there are other little recreational clubs to join, like the Hash House Harriers running group, CI Arts and Culture, the golf club, CI Cricket and Sporting Club, volleyball and the odd book club. There is plenty to do and see and people are very social, it can be a very active place to live and an amazing place to raise kids.

The other main service on the island is the Indian Ocean Territories Health Service (IOTHS). This is a commonwealth funded health service including both Christmas Island and the Cocos (Keeling) Islands and was my workplace. The health service is administered by the Department of Regional Australia (DoRA) which is a non-health related department. This is where service administration comes undone because it's like having funeral directors run a restaurant, it just doesn't really make sense because it's not their area of expertise.

The Christmas Island health service was an amazing little service, for the first few years they conducted all chest x-rays for new boat arrivals and the corridors were lined with asylum seekers waiting their turn. The chest x-rays were mostly conducted by the highly skilled Enrolled nurses who often identified bullets and shrapnel left from warfare. Many people were treated for active Tuberculosis or other infectious diseases needing isolation for a minimum fourteen-day admission, before being returned to the detention environment. IHMS provided the general medical clinic work in the detention centre but any emergency treatment such as suturing wounds, setting fractures, cardiac arrests and general medical admissions were managed by IOTHS. Needless to say, the place was incredibly busy and the medical staff worked hard with little recognition. The medical expertise in a tiny eight-bedroom hospital was astounding and the interesting medical presentations relied on a high skill mix. The GPs and nursing staff on the floor were also called on to care for survivors of boat disasters such as the horror of SIEV 221 on the morning of 15 December 2010, when the island witnessed the death of fifty men, women and children in huge swells. There were twenty bodies never retrieved as an indication of the extreme sea conditions and the thirty bodies located were kept on the IOTHS grounds in refrigerated shipping containers for months. The containers lined the staff driveway and were a daily reminder of the horrors of the sea. To some local staff the containers were very disturbing due to cultural superstitions and beliefs, and this made coming to work difficult. The next time bodies needed to be stored for an extended period of time they were stored in the police yard, hidden behind hessian screening.

There were other disasters and emergencies the IOTHS staff dealt with such as car accidents, suicides, self-harming, psychotic episodes, women in labour, sick babies, they had it all. Additionally, the islands are visited by specialists such as a paediatrician, gynaecologist, radiographer, speech pathologist and physiotherapist, while any surgery is done on the mainland, in Perth. Emergencies are met by a Medivac off the island, after hospital staff stabilise a patient, sometimes for hours waiting for the medical flight.

Another important island service is the local police force provided by the AFP, with police generally sourced from Canberra for a two-year posting into the community policing team. The additional AFP force on the island changed to reflect the situation at the time, the riot squad were present at times and the people smuggling team were used in the days when asylum processing occurred on the island. But it was the community police who worked alongside Customs, Navy, IOTHS and the volunteer ambos and marine rescue in response to several boat disasters and they were exposed to some horrific scenes, a far cry from mainstream Canberra life.

Directed outings

When the T&T team first started we discovered there were about six members of the Christmas Island community people who were granted access to take people out of detention. When we enquired about this, we were told that people can apply to the Department of Immigration to become a *directed person*. A directed person is granted the authority to take people out of detention and during that specified time the asylum seeker is under their guardianship. Of course it has to be taken very seriously and our team all applied to become directed persons, which we found was a great reward to our clients and to us.

Taking people on a directed outing was a great opportunity to connect with the clients and get to know them very well. After some time, we would take out a whole family or a group of friends and what made it truly wonderful was we didn't have to be escorted by a Serco officer. In our government issued four-wheeled drives, we would go and collect people from detention and sign them into our care, we tried to do a directed outing once a fortnight sometimes it might be for a couple of hours or for a full day. We were limited due to our always huge waiting list and our client caseloads from taking too much time away from the office. The other people who took asylum seekers out regularly were the Catholic nuns sent over to the island under an arrangement between the Jesuit Refugee Service (JRS) in Sydney and the Department of Immigration. When I first arrived Sister Joan was the nun who worked tirelessly for months on end with a bottomless pit of compassion, she was truly amazing. She was followed by Lizzy, Rita, Dorothy and Margaret, they are all incredible women. Dorothy had dedicated her life as a nun working as a nurse midwife in Africa and Papua New Guinea, she has enough stories for an epic motion picture. An incredibly hardworking and practical person Dorothy initially struggled to accept that offering support through acts of kindness and words was enough and she exhausted herself racing around the compounds to see as many people as she could. She is aged in her seventies and I am sure won't stop until she drops. When she left the island, she spent time on Nauru and then managed to convince her boss, the reverend mother, to allow her to go back to work in Africa where she has set up a medical clinic in a remote impoverished area of Sudan.

Sister Margaret is a teacher and was instrumental in getting the six months of quality education happening on the island. These women came to the island as solo workers to provide pastoral care and were also *directed persons.* Immigration made up lists of random people for them to take out and they would take them around for picnics and a walk, and allow families a chance to be together in a moment of freedom. They also paid for countless ice-creams and drinks out of their own pockets and will probably be cringing as I acknowledge the good work they did. Mother Teresa was spot on when she said *kind words can be short and easy to speak, but their echoes are truly endless* what these beautiful women offered to hundreds of men and women and children was great solace.

The directed outings granted access for traumatised people to breathe freely again, to walk outside the prison-like walls and to actually feel human. Invariably people would be whistling or singing within half an hour, I would normally bake something homemade for lunch and pack a thermos and a big picnic because it was important for me to let people know that they were worthy. We'd go and see some beautiful sites and do some short jungle walks, but really it was just about providing an opportunity for people to heal and to offer decency.

Ali

On many occasions I would ask in a session for someone to tell me about their happy memories or for a single happy occasion in their life. As part of therapy we would talk about that occasion and I would encourage people to believe they would have similar occasions in the future as a pathway to hope. This technique worked well until I met thirty-two-year-old Ali. I remember feeling so sad for this man when he told me he didn't have any happy memories and I knew that he wasn't saying this to seek attention, he was genuine. I decided that I needed to create a moment of happiness, a memory for him to hold onto. I booked a directed outing for Ali and an interpreter, something I never normally bothered with but as he was a single male I thought it would be more comfortable and appropriate for him to have the interpreter there. I baked late into the night to provide a special feast and packed a picnic with real crockery, cutlery and a tablecloth, everything needed for an honoured guest. The three of us had an incredible day because the weather was perfect, the food was great, the ocean was calm, and the island was magnificent in its beauty. Nearing the end of the day we were standing at a lookout called Margaret Knoll, which is high up looking over the top of the jungle and out to a beautiful ocean view and Ali smiled. This was a huge authentic smile, one that shines from the inside out, he turned to me and said *this is the happiest day of my life, this is happiness!* On the drive home from North West Point I couldn't play loud music, I didn't play a quiet ballad, I just had to have silence on that drive, I found it so incredibly tragic that I really just wanted to cry. I had managed to create in a few short hours one man's happiest day of his life and I found that to be powerfully sad.

On another directed outing my colleague agreed to do a joint outing for a large Iraqi family, when we went to pick up the family we discovered that one of the kids was celebrating her birthday. On Christmas Island there is a roundabout surrounded by blackboards, it's where the locals put all the community announcements including birthdays, so while my colleague drove through the roundabout ahead of me with the birthday girl in her car, I pulled in and wrote up a happy sixteenth birthday sign. When we came back through the roundabout we did laps around and around so the family could all see it, they were delighted. On another occasion I took out three young unaccompanied minors who had travelled all the way from Somalia, when I picked them up they were quite guarded but it didn't take long before they were giggling and absolutely loving it. The highlight for them on this occasion was chasing giant Coconut crabs, known as *Robber crabs* off the road and picking limes from the trees at Grants Well in the centre of the island.

On many occasions I would have my client nominate their three best friends or roommates, this meant that I would often be taking out people that I'd never met before. I tried to avoid taking interpreters unless I really needed to, because I figured that if people can communicate their needs to Serco guards for a year or two they most certainly could communicate with me for a few hours tripping around the island. It wasn't unusual to find when I picked up some of these random friends of clients, that they had been detained for up to twelve months or more without leaving the detention centre. The outing was the first time they had left the detention centre since arriving on the island and their only opportunity to be treated as if they were not criminal. My colleagues and I talked about the impact of these outings on many occasions and we all identified what we described as a physical shift within the car as we neared the detention centre. The clients had to mentally prepare themselves for the return to detainment and it would often leave us feeling helpless. One girl described it as putting on her *coat of sadness*, when she left the centre she felt physically lighter because she left her coat at the gate, but returning meant putting the coat back on. We all received so much positive feedback from our clients after these outings, to me they instilled hope and it doesn't need to be more meaningful than that.

It was just short of my fifth year on Christmas Island when my colleagues and I were given just four weeks' notice that our service was no longer required. We suddenly had to plan how we would best utilise our last month, of course it wasn't going to be adding new assessments and new clients to our list because there is no therapeutic value in doing that. Asking someone to share their story and then offering no way to heal is pointless, so we were intent on farewelling our current clients and their friends and families properly. Until we were suddenly denied the right to take our clients on directed outings. We each received a directive that highlighted the punitive nature of working with public servants and the enormous negative impact one disgruntled public servant can have on client care. The situation between our service and Immigration on Christmas Island was tense to say the least and the HLO wanted to have the last say by imposing a punishment or a slap on the wrist to show who's in control. We had been considered too vocal in our opposition to the failings in the detention system and were to be punished. It was our clients who received that punishment, not us, how very different our farewells could have been if we had been granted access to the last walk on the beach with them and their friends and families, that last offer of kindness.

Client impressions

For most clients being detained equated to being imprisoned for a criminal act and they were genuinely confused by the length of the detainment and the very harsh restrictions placed on them. It was understood by most people arriving by boat that they would be detained, however they didn't realise that detainment would be for two years or more. They justifiably thought that they would be held for a matter of weeks. There was an expectation of security and medical checks, and an assumption they would be released into the community for processing, as is done in every other country that takes asylum seekers and refugees. A common complaint was the not knowing, people would say that they would be better off in a prison, at least that way you knew your length of sentence and could know what you had to wait out. Our whole team often struggled to explain the reasons for decisions made or treatment meted out by immigration and Serco. One example we all found disturbing was when a boy turned eighteen he would be removed from his family and taken to North West Point to reside with all the single adult males. I knew of one boy who was moved on his actual eighteenth birthday and the family was understandably distressed. It was impossible to rationalise a decision that saw a child living with his family as a typical seventeen-year-old suddenly be seen as unfit to be in the same compound as his family overnight. We had questions directed at us by our clients that we simply could not answer, it seemed decisions did not have to make sense or be humane within a detention centre.

When speaking to Hakim a young Afghan man released after eighteen months in detention, he told me that there were many inconsistencies while he was detained, for example he was never interviewed by the AFP, yet everyone else he knew had at least one interview with them. He also had only four brief appointments with immigration during the entire eighteen months. He wasn't complaining in any way, but he was confused by the inconsistent process, he said that *you lose every day your mind in detention* and that the constant reminders by immigration of a pending transfer to Manus Island or to Nauru depleted hope. He said that gradually over time everyone will be affected in some negative way from detainment, no matter how strong they are.

Survival

For my own survival I had to find a way to balance my intense workload with parenting and endless social activities. I joined the Hash House Harriers as a very *slow runner* and I also loved to escape to remote locations to camp and my favourite spot was Dolly Beach. Bella and I had hammock tents that we hanged between coconut palms right on the beach, we watched giant turtles coming up to lay their eggs, turtle hatchlings making their way down to the water, and we swam with whale sharks and dolphins, and experienced the majesty of the red crab migration. I also loved going four-wheel driving around the island and taking long hikes in the jungle with my machete in hand, it was so much fun hacking my way through the dense jungle. I joined a book club and was the secretary of the outdoor cinema club for three years, I really loved being able to sit outside under the stars and the rain watching a movie.

I also found food for the soul at the Christmas Island Catholic church which was the first place Bella and I visited the day after we arrived. This was not because I am deeply religious, but because we were woken very early by the island's roosters and I thought that it might not be a bad place to start our island adventure, plus it would please my Dad. Dad had not long retired and had taken himself to the local community resource centre back home to learn how to use a computer, he googled the Christmas Island church and informed me that *mass was on at nine o'clock on Sunday morning.* The church held a weekly service and offered mass whenever a priest visited. This little church community became so incredibly special to me, it was made up of quirky characters that you couldn't make up in your wildest dreams and this mixed bag of people helped me stay focused on doing good work. Built on the hillside with a spectacular view over the ocean, it was not unusual to arrive at church to see a refugee boat had arrived in the cove or to see a plume of black smoke out on the horizon indicating the Navy had destroyed another refugee boat and were sending it as a burnt offering to the bottom of the ocean. The gardens leading up the hillside surrounding the little church were spectacular and tended with great love and devotion by the old Chinese man known as Cowboy. Cowboy was also Santa Claus at the Christmas celebration each year and would arrive on the back of the local fire truck ringing a hand-held bell, it was definitely the most animated I would see him. I had been told that the local travel agent Gee Foo believed she had a received a vision from Our Lady instructing her to ensure the church should honour the virgin mother. Gee poured a lot of time, money and devotion into the maintenance of the gardens and in about 2012 included several ornate lighted trees that glowed bright pink, orange and blue, there was also a lime green palm tree making these gardens hilariously unique. Each year on the anniversary of the Virgin Marys assumption into heaven and also on her birthday we had a vigil in the evening, we would light small tea candles to line the stone path and steps leading up the hillside to a grotto, I always found this incredibly spiritual.

Bella made her first Holy Communion in the church and was an angel in the Christmas pageant and I sang off key in the Christmas choir each year, with the singing each week working as a tonic for another week. When we didn't have a priest, Ron or his generous wife Susan would deliver the service and Paul or his majestic wife Glenda would often read the gospel. Dear Cowboy would be very put out if he was not the last to shuffle bare foot up the tiny aisle to receive Holy Communion and everyone always adopted their expected role. As Celestine belted out a song on his guitar, his wife Lucia would be singing her lungs out whilst Monica would add her voice to the chorus as she also placed yet more flowers on the altar and a cacophony of sound would bring a song to a screeching finale.

The Jesuit Refugee Service coordinated volunteer priests to visit, particularly in 2010 and 2011 when the detention centre was packed with Sri Lankan Catholics. Having a priest to visit and conduct a mass every week was very important to them and so the little local catholic community also benefited. I met some wonderful priests who came from diverse backgrounds often having worked in missions in Africa, South East Asia and beyond. Each Sunday at the church Serco would bring a bus of different asylum seekers along for the service, the readings were always delivered in English and then in Chinese but they also added one or two other languages depending who was there. It always re-energised me just watching and listening to the gospel read out in Tamil or Farsi because it was about respect and compassion for each and when we were all in the church there was no *us* and *them*. I will never forget the first time I heard a large group of men singing The Lord's Prayer in Tamil. I felt that they were going to lift the roof off the little church with such passion and devotion, it was very emotional. We also had some Vietnamese asylum seekers detained on the island for over twelve months, they regularly attended and harmonised beautifully together and when they read the gospel it was a beautiful melody. I don't want to give a false impression, I am certainly no angel, like most people that do intense hard work, I partied hard, drank a lot and ate far too much, but I was lucky I developed a great network of supportive friends and I have always had my family present in the background.

Lessons learnt

By May 2014 our T&T service was suffering and it did not help that the Director of the Department of Regional Australia (DoRA) governing the island was irritated with me and our service. This irritation had stemmed firstly from an event where he felt humiliated by my team, when during an Indian Ocean Territories staff award ceremony he was publicly corrected after referring to people seeking asylum as *those illegals*. And secondly, by my personal association with the island administrator Jon Stanhope, it was no secret that the two men had clashed with their views of the world and opinion of refugees and people seeking asylum being polar opposite. Jon had accepted the position of Administrator of the Indian Ocean Territories following a political career that saw him hold the position of Chief Minister of the ACT from 2001 to 2011. He is a well-known advocate for human rights and wanted to develop an informed opinion of the treatment of people seeking asylum on Christmas Island we saw each other socially and he was very supportive of the work our service provided.

In an effort to improve the staff moral I suggested to the team we plan activities to recognise refugee week scheduled for the third week of June. I had either organised an event or participated in some way in previous years and now more than ever I felt we needed something positive to work on with our clients and the island community. The theme for Refugee Week was *Restoring Hope* and that was exactly what I wanted to achieve so I contacted Jon to see if he would join us in organising the events. We planned an art exhibition to be displayed during the week at a local restaurant known as *The Chinese Literary Association*. Jon was set to officially open the event and the local school was on board with kids making their master pieces ready to exhibit, as were many men, women and children in the detention centre. I was also working on a painting of my own I was determined the week was to promote positivity, so there was a strict guideline to stick to the theme, the artwork was to be bright, positive and hopeful. Jon helped to organise a day on the golf course with local golfers set to partner an asylum seeker, National Parks were keen to do a day of tree planting together and we planned a family fun day at the cricket oval for the local community and families in detention with old fashioned egg and spoon and sack races. It was only one week before the event that I received word from both the directors of DoRA and Immigration that the events were to be cancelled, no asylum seekers were to be allowed to participate. The reason given was that it was a celebration of no relevance to the *detainees* because they were *illegal asylum seekers*, not refugees and we were not to give them any hope. I can relate to the idiom *the straw that broke the camel's back* this was my final straw, I was forced to cancel each event and phone all the people in the community including my team and my clients, I was completely deflated. Adding to our stress was an unstable future, our employment contracts were due to expire in November and although the funding from the Department of Immigration had been extended in May to allow for future contract extensions, DoRA was delaying the renewal of our contracts.

I was feeling increasingly undermined by the oppressive and covert treatment directed at us by the Department of Immigration, we had limited dialogue and what we were told was often through subterfuge. The island is a place always alive with rumours, the one we kept hearing was that the detention centre was to be permanently closed and all asylum seekers would be sent off to Nauru or Manus Island, we had no way of knowing if this was going to happen or if it was in fact idle gossip. Meanwhile the Department of Immigration had gradually reduced and restricted our ability to provide clinical recommendations for our clients, with the dreaded Immigration Privacy Policy quoted at us incessantly, we were being shut out of communication and the ability to advocate for our clients. Never had our opposing ethics been more evident than at this time, there was an irrational level of fear among the detention workforce that saw shameful decisions over a person's health and wellbeing made without question or debate. The HLO at the time relished her power to remove the limited dialogue we had remaining within the detention network and made it a personal vendetta to diminish our team. I was alarmed to find that IHMS were directed to limit their once open dialogue with us, leading them to become guarded and suspicious, I was also personally hurt by their willingness to take such a directive without question. By this time, we had already been directed not to liaise with the school teachers about our client's wellbeing, we were very constrained to provide restricted care.

In October, we each received an email from the Director of DoRA advising that our service was no longer required, he did this without discussion with the Department of Immigration. When I contacted Detention Health in Canberra they were unaware and clearly embarrassed by the blunder, I dialled into a conference call to detention health in Canberra and heard the throat clearing and stuttering of a man who was obviously unimpressed by the directive we had received. They advised the DoRA director to offer me and another staff member to stay on contract, we declined. I was deeply offended that a team of clinicians could be treated with such disrespect, we had four weeks to pack up and close down our service and decided that the clients on our case lists would be given a dignified last few weeks of therapy.

Although we still had a large number of people on the waiting list for service, our right to access the Nominal roll and transfer lists had long been removed, we had no way to check if people were still on the island and no way of knowing the exact number of people on the list. We determined that starting sessions with a new client would be of no therapeutic value and that our energy should be focussed on our current caseloads and community clients. The HLO emailed a directive that our presence at the CPPM meetings was no longer required so any clinical recommendations could be emailed to her and we were not able to discuss our clinical concerns. We wanted to take our clients out for directed outings with friends or family to give them hope and a gracious closure, but this was also denied when our right to conduct the outings were refused. The explanation provided was that there were many people still on the waiting list for counselling therefore we couldn't possibly be spending time taking clients out on outings, it was a deliberate last kick in the guts for each of us.

During the final two weeks on the island I was faced with a challenge to our team's professional integrity, we heard another rumour but this time is made my blood boil. Our professional practice was being discredited, someone had been suggesting that we had been coaching clients to self-harm to enable a transfer to the mainland. It was suspiciously similar to the unfounded allegations made toward the *Save the Children's* workers on Nauru, but we had only a rumour and nothing written or verbalised publicly. I was incensed because the implication that we were coaching clients was both hideous and ludicrous, we were so intent on providing a pathway to healing for each of clients and we took our work very seriously. A rumour such as this had the capacity to ruin our professional credibility and was evidently a very deliberate and a shameful end to our service, the dreaded *white-anting* had begun. During our last week the Department of Immigration directed DoRA to send two trauma counsellors from the mainland to maintain a counselling service. When our little team dismantled and left the island we were all battered and bruised by the final treatment meted out, for me personally I have taken time to heal. When people suggest the trauma content of the work must have been difficult to deal with, I have always countered that it wasn't the trauma stories, it was the relentless battle with Immigration policy, procedures and public servants.

I had spent years nursing in a variety of settings, some remote and sometimes dangerous, but I had remained naive when it came to the lack of morality in politics and inner workings of government departments, because I had always worked for a healthcare organisation or aid agency with compassionate values. I had wrongly assumed that people in general, are considerate of others and that we Australians are particularly caring because we recognise how lucky we are, but I was wrong. Five years of torture and trauma counselling on the frontline provided great insight and I came away from Christmas Island with disturbing awareness into the workings of government. I witnessed the painful reality created when governments are determined to use humanity for political purpose and I have learnt that public servants, politicians and policy makers do not care about individual human life. It took time for me to grasp that for many people the lives of a few desperate people don't really amount to much unless there is political gain.

I also recognise the majority of Australians remain ill-informed of our government's policies and practices and that most people don't think to inquire. I found that most Australians are more than happy to gain their limited knowledge of important local and world issues from horrendous shock-jocks and trashy tabloid editorials. They are unaware these views are politically driven and when informed are not particularly bothered. True political discussion is frowned upon as an indication that a person is a *bloody leftie* but what does that actually mean in 2018, to me it feels that we are no better off than we were in the 1950s; that we haven't evolved. To do my bit, I have been speaking publicly of my experiences on the island since I returned to the mainland. I faced the challenge of breaching the secrecy provisions of the Border Force Act when they were introduced in 2015 and was very active in successfully petitioning to repeal the abhorrent legislation. The success from that has given me hope, I have not been silent however it's not always easy to find a new audience, I find that I am often preaching to the converted and although I love their support they are not who I want to address.

And now, I have written this memoir because I hope to provide a clearer understanding of the reasons why people have journeyed so far to seek asylum and to allow a glimpse into life in Immigration detention on Christmas Island. But these memories didn't come easily, there have been elements of the recollections that I had not allowed myself to process during my time on Christmas Island because it was just too hard and I was psychologically protecting myself. The process of writing and remembering has been huge for me, but in a positive cathartic way. I did battle with an obvious ethical conflict before I started writing as these are personal narratives shared in confidence in a therapeutic space, I needed to be certain that I was not abusing my power by telling the stories of the less powerful. But I reasoned that I have a moral obligation to share this information because I want to make the less powerful, The Powerful. I have told the truth because anything less would be completely dishonourable and pointless, these stories don't need exaggeration because they can't be made any more tragic and painful than they already are. They are true narratives shared with me by some of the hundreds of men, women and children that I have had the privilege to meet; to each, I honour you.

Epilogue: It Is Written in Our Destiny

Only two weeks after we returned to the mainland I received a phone call *Hello, how are you? This is Omid* and so began a new chapter in my life, when Omid joined our family. At twenty-one years of age Omid fled the Taliban in Afghanistan and made his way to Australia, arriving by boat on Christmas Island he soon discovered he was not going to be heading to Australia anytime soon. The majority of people off his boat were sent to Manus Island where many still remain, Omid cannot explain why he was not sent to Manus Island, or why he was chosen to be sent to a counsellor after being detained on the island for twelve months. Or why he was allocated to my list on that day and how it came to be that I gave him my contact details in case he ever needed them in the future. He will always say that *it is written in our destiny* and I am starting to believe in his simple philosophy.

When he appeared for the first session on Christmas Island he was completely bewildered as to why he had been sent to see me, he told me that he was doing well, staying very active playing volleyball as much as he could. I instantly liked him because he was so alive and vibrant, he was trying out his limited English language skills and was very confident. In the detention centre the other men were impressed by Omid's command of the English language, they would regularly call on him to act as their interpreter with the Serco guards in the compound. This had given Omid a false sense that he was fluent in the language and it bolstered his confidence. He is naturally positive and this provides an impressive level of resilience however he was worried, he asked *how do I stop myself from going mad like everyone else?* It was that simple question that connected with me, I knew that I had the ability to keep this boy well by simply bringing him into our service each week for a chat and adding him and his friends to a directed outing once and while, so that's what I did.

During his detainment on Christmas Island he developed a problem with his jaw, he saw the doctor on a number of occasions and then quite miraculously he found himself on a medical transfer flight to Darwin. Believe me when I say how miraculous this is because there was always a huge number of men, women and children suffering relentlessly on a medical transfer waitlist. When Omid failed to attend a weekly session, I assumed he had been transferred to Manus Island. So, when I took the call in December 2014 I was surprised when he told me had been released from detention in Darwin just the day before and flown to Brisbane on a Bridging Visa. He was given temporary accommodation in an old motel along with several other men, they were linked with a case worker and told to find their own accommodation as soon as possible. After chatting to him I wished him well and told him how delighted I was to hear from him and to discover that he had not been sent to Manus Island.

Over the course of the next three days I received more phone calls from Omid, usually he was wandering lost in the streets of Brisbane, each call came with growing anxiety and fear. I realised that if this was my daughter Bella in a foreign country with only one contact in her phone list I would want that person to care for her. I directed Omid to find the nearest public library knowing there would be access to free computers to set up a Gmail account, I emailed a one-way ticket to Melbourne and Bella and I borrowed my brothers' car to pick him up at Tullamarine airport. We were standing in the airport waiting for his plane to arrive when we saw this thin, frightened boy walk towards us, he was visibly shaking. There had been a young

Aussie bloke sitting beside Omid on the flight, they must have struck up conversation and it was evident that this stranger was looking out for him, he deliberately walked off slowly to make sure Omid was going to be met by someone, he gave me a look of recognition with a quick nod and smile, then he was on his way. This simple act of kindness has stayed with me.

Omid has become a member of our family, Bella looks to him like a special big brother, he reprimands Bella like a big protective brother should and I feel blessed to have him in my life. Omid has managed to master the English language, graduate high school and be awarded a scholarship to study bio-medical science at university. He has fallen in love and just become engaged to be married, he is still waiting for the outcome of his asylum claim. The application for a Safe Haven Enterprise Visa has been lodged and we are all waiting to see if this will be granted, it will only give him the right to stay for five years at a time.

Just recently we were shopping in Dandenong where there is an established Afghan community and some of the best Afghan shopping in Melbourne. We were looking for a new traditional outfit for Omid's engagement ceremony when we were over heard by a young Afghan woman. She introduced herself as Maryam and told us that her mother sews from home, she gave us her phone number in case we couldn't find what we wanted. Later that day we went to her house and met her mother Khadija who kindly measured Omid up for his clothes, as I chatted to Maryam I gave her my email address and we left. Later that evening I received an email from Maryam she said she realised that I must have been the same Christine Cummins who had counselled many people on Christmas Island. Her mother had attended an Afghan women's group that I had run, she said the women still get together and they sometimes talk about me and their time on the island. I was really excited to receive the email it was beautiful and it validated that the work I did had made an impact. I recalled that my parents had visited us on Christmas Island back in 2011 and that my Mum had joined one of the Afghan women's groups. The ladies had been so excited to meet my Mum, the next week they presented her with some handmade paper flowers, she was really touched by this kind gesture and carried the flowers back home to country Victoria in a shoebox. When I told Omid this story he mentioned it to Khadija when he picked up his clothes. He said my Grandma was presented with some flowers, Khadija said *I know she was, I was the one who made them.*

Home by Warsan Shire

No one leaves home unless home is the mouth of a shark
You only run for the border when you see the whole city running as well
Your neighbours running faster than you breath, bloody in their throats
The boy you went to school with who kissed you dizzy behind the old tin factory is holding a gun bigger than his body
You only leave home when home won't let you stay.
No one leaves home unless home chases you fire under feet hot blood in your belly, it's not
something you ever thought of doing until the blade burnt threats into your neck and even
then you carried the anthem under your breath,
only tearing up your passport in an airport toilet, sobbing as each mouthful of paper made it clear that you wouldn't be going back.
You have to understand, that no one puts their children in a boat unless the water is safer than the land.
No one burns their palms under trains, beneath carriages
No one spends days and nights in the stomach of a truck feeding on newspaper unless the miles travelled means something more than journey.
No one crawls under fences
No one wants to be beaten, pitied
No one chooses refugee camps or strip searches where your body is left aching
Or prison, because prison is safer than a city of fire and one prison guard in the night is better
than a truckload of men who look like your father

No one could take it
No one could stomach it
No one skin would be tough enough
The go home blacks, Refugees, Dirty immigrants, Asylum seekers sucking our country dry,
Niggers with their hands out, they smell strange
Savage, messed up their country and now they want to mess ours up
How do the words, the dirty looks roll off your backs
Maybe because the blow is softer than a limb torn off
Or the words are more tender than fourteen men between your legs
Or the insults are easier to swallow than rubble, than bone, than your child body in pieces.
I want to go home, but home is the mouth of a shark
Home is the barrel of the gun and no one would leave home unless home chased you to the
shore
Unless home told you to quicken your legs, leave your clothes behind, crawl through the
desert, wade through the oceans
Drown
Save
Be hunger
Beg
Forget pride, your survival is more important
No one leaves home until home is a sweaty voice in your ear
Saying leave, run away from me now
I don't know what I've become but I know that anywhere is safer than here.

Names and Their Meanings

The names of all clients have been deliberately changed to a name with a meaning reflecting each person as I remember them.

Peter: A rock
Mathuran: Leader
Joseph: God will add
Lavinia: Working for peace
Sylvia: Beautiful silver flower
Chajan: Deep thinker
Kimaya: Miracle
Mustafa: The chosen one
Abdullah: Servant of God
Reza: Contentment
Morteza: Chosen
Saman: Elegant
Maryam: Wished for
Zareb: Protector against enemies
Ruhi: Spiritual
Fatima: Captivating
Tasmeen: Strong
Maheer: Brave
Majid: Glorious
Azmi: Strong
Amal: Hope

Jamila: Beautiful
Behnam: Honourable
Mohammad: Glorified
Aktar: Good man
Amina: Trustworthy
Habib: Beloved
Mohsen: Humanitarian
Dinanath: Protector
Naji: Survivor
Raj: Ruler
Asha: Hope
Rani: Queen
Kumaran: Youthful
Adel: Righteous
Ehsan: Compassion
Matthew: Gift of the lord
Vani: God's gift
Bishaaro: Delight or Joy
Sevvi: Strong person
Pratheesh: Hope
Rashid: Rightly guided
Pramada: Beautiful lady
Panbu: Good character
Bala: Young
Afeef: Pure
Hakim: Wise
Ali: Noble
Omid: Hope

Acronyms

AGD	Attorney General's Department
AFP	Australian Federal Police
ALIV	Australian League of Immigration Volunteers
ASIO	Australian Security Intelligence Organisation
CIDHS	Christmas Island District High School
CC	Construction Camp (Detention facility for families)
CPPM	Client Placement and Preventative Meeting
CID	Criminal Investigation Department (Sri Lanka)
DIAC	Department of Immigration and Citizenship
DIBP	Department of Immigration and Border Protection
DIMIA	Department of Immigration and Multicultural and Indigenous Affairs
DoRA	Department of Regional Australia
DeHAG	Detention Health Advisory Group
DPPM	Detainee Placement and Preventative Meeting
EAP	Employee Assistance Program
ERT	Emergency Response Team (Serco)
FASSTT	Forum of Australian Services for Survivors of Torture and Trauma
HLO	Health Liaison Officer
IDC	Immigration Detention Centre
IHAG	Immigration Health Advisory Group
IHMS	International Health and Medical Service
IMR	Independent Merit Review
IOM	International Organisation for Migration
IOTHS	Indian Ocean Territories Health Service
JRS	Jesuit Refugee Service

LTTE	Liberation Tigers of Tamil Eelam (Tamil Tigers)
MOU	Memorandum of Understanding
MSF	Médecins Sans Frontières
NAATI	National Accreditation Authority for Translators and Interpreters
NGO	Non-Government Organisation
NWP	North West Point (location of the Christmas Island Immigration Detention Centre)
OSB	Operation Sovereign Borders
RPC	Regional Processing Centre
RSA	Refugee Status Assessment
SDA	Service Delivery Agreement
SIEV	Suspected Illegal Entry Vessel
TB	Tuberculosis
T&E	Transport and Escort (Serco)
T&T	Torture and Trauma
UAM	Unaccompanied Minor
UN	United Nations
UNHCR	United Nations High Commission for Refugees

Militia Groups

Al Shabab is an Islamist militant group in Somalia, banned as a terrorist group by both the US and the UK and is believed to have between 7,000 and 9,000 fighters. Al Shabab advocates the Saudi-inspired Wahhabi version of Islam imposing a strict version of Sharia in areas under its control, this includes stoning to death women accused of adultery and amputating the hands of thieves.

Al Mahdi Army is a Shia paramilitary group in Iraq, members of the Al Mahdi Army frequently carried out atrocities, particularly against Sunni civilians. The Al Mahdi Army has also been accused of operating death squads.

Basji, the Basij Resistance Force is a volunteer paramilitary organisation operating under the Islamic Revolutionary Guards Corps in Iran. It is an auxiliary force with many duties, especially internal security, law enforcement, special religious or political events and morals policing. The Basij have branches in virtually every city and town in Iran and are religious fundamentalists.

Sepah is the common name for the Army of the Guardians of the Islamic Revolution, often called Revolutionary Guards or Islamic Revolutionary Guard Corps. They are another Iranian fundamentalist group that state their role is protecting the Islamic system and preventing foreign interference as well as coups by the military or 'deviant movements'.

Taliban is a Sunni Islamic fundamentalist political movement that emerged in the early 1990s in northern Pakistan following the withdrawal of Soviet troops from Afghanistan. They are an Islamic movement that has proved to be a formidable fighting force in Afghanistan and a major threat to its government. They continue to mount frequent suicide bombings and other attacks across the country targeting civilians who do not conform to their ideology.

ISIS, also known as the Islamic State of Iraq and Syria and by its Arabic language acronym Daesh. It is widely known for its videos of beheadings of both soldiers and civilians, including journalists and aid workers, and its destruction of cultural heritage sites. The United Nations holds ISIS responsible for human rights abuses and war crimes, and Amnesty International has charged the group with ethnic cleansing on a historic scale in northern Iraq and Syria.

The Liberation Tigers of Tamil Eelam, commonly known as the LTTE or the Tamil Tigers was a Tamil militant organisation that was based in north eastern Sri Lanka. Founded in 1976 by Velupillai Prabhakaran, it waged a secessionist nationalist insurgency to create an independent state of Tamil Eelam in the north and east of Sri Lanka for Tamil people. This campaign led to the Sri Lankan Civil War, which ran from 1983 until 2009 when the LTTE was defeated by the Sri Lankan military.

The Kurdistan Free Life Party or **PJAK** is a Kurdish political and militant organisation which has waged an intermittent armed struggle since 2004 against the Iranian government to seek self-determination for Kurds in Iranian Kurdistan.

The Free Syrian Army was founded in 2011 by officers who defected from the Syrian Armed Forces who said their goal was to bring down the government of Bashar al-Assad. It has adopted guerrilla-style tactics in the countryside and cities. The campaign is not meant to hold territory, but rather, to spread government forces and their logistics chains thin in battles for urban centres, to cause slow destruction to the security forces, to degrade morale and to destabilise Damascus, the centre of government.

Notes

1. United Nations Convention and Protocol relating to the Status of Refugees (1951), http://www.unhcr.org/en-au/1951-refugee-convention.html.
2. Asylum Seeker Resource Centre. (2014). *Asylum seekers and Refugees, myths, facts and solutions,* https://www.asrc.org.au/pdf/myths-facts-solutions-info_.pdf.
3. United Nations High Commission for Refugees Midyear Trends (2015), http://www.unhcr.org/en-au/statistics/unhcrstats/56701b969/mid-year-trends-june-2015.html?query=mid%20year%20trends.
4. Sri Lanka: growing UN concern as civilians in 'safe zone' come under fire, 17 February 2009, http://www.un.org/apps/news/story.asp?NewsID=29922#.WBgdEuB95.
5. Report of the Commission of inquiry on Lessons Learnt and Reconciliation (2011), http://www.priu.gov.lk/news_update/Current_Affairs/ca201112/FINAL%20LLRC%20RE PORT.pdf.
6. Selye, Hans (1956). *The Stress of Life.* New York, NY, US: McGraw-Hill, p. 324.
7. Unrepresented nations and people's organization (2014). *Ethnic and Religious Minorities in Iran*, http://unpo.org/downloads/936.pdf.
8. Centre for religious pluralism in the Middle East. *The Continuous persecution in Iran: Ahwaz as a model*, 6 July 2016, http://www.crpme.gr/analysis/iran/the-continuous-persecution-in-iran-ahwaz-as-a-model.
9. Aziz, Y. (2012). Al Arabiya News. *What do Arabs of Iran want?* Retrieved from https://english.alarabiya.net/views/2012/09/23/239607.html.

10. Human Rights Watch. *Prisoners of the Past Kuwaiti Bidun and the Burden of Statelessness* (2011), https://www.hrw.org/report/2011/06/13/prisoners-past/kuwaiti-bidun-and-burden-statelessness.
11. United Nations High Commission for Refugees Midyear Trends. (2015), http://www.unhcr.org/en-au/statistics/unhcrstats/56701b969/mid-year-trends-june-2015.html?query=mid%20year%20trends.
12. Masters, J., Sergie, M. A. (2015). Al-Shabab. *Council on Foreign Relations*, http://www.cfr.org/somalia/al-shabab/p18650.
13. Coelho, P. (1998). *The Alchemist.* New York: Harper Collins.
14. Palmer, M. (2005). *Inquiry into the Circumstances of the Immigration Detention of Cornelia Rau.* Palmer Report, http://www.minister.immi.gov.au/media_releases/media05/palmer-report.pdf.
15. Comrie, N. (2005). *Inquiry into the Circumstances of the Vivian Alvarez Matter.* Comrie Report, http://www.ombudsman.gov.au/publications_information/Special_Reports/2005/alvarez_report 03.pdf.
16. Parliament of Australia (2013). *Need for independent oversight of health services*, http://www.aph.gov.au/Parliamentary_Business/Committees/Senate/Legal_and_Constitutional_Affairs/Completed_inquiries/2010-13/migrationhealthcare2012/report/c02.
17. Australian Medical Association (2013). *AMA shocked by disbanding of Immigration Health Advisory Group (IHAG)*, https://ama.com.au/media/ama-shocked-disbanding-immigration-health-advisory-group-ihag.
18. Department of Immigration and Citizenship (2011). *Christmas Island – North-West Point Immigration Detention Centre Client Placement and Preventative Meeting guidelines.*
19. Honoré de Balzac (1834). *Le Père Goriot*, http://www.goodreads.com/quotes/222564-behind-every-great-fortune-there-is-a-crime.
20. Hawke, A., Williams, H. (2011). *Independent Review of the Incidents at the Christmas Island Immigration Detention Centre and Villawood Immigration Detention Centre*, https://www.border.gov.

au/ReportsandPublications/Documents/reviews-and-inquiries/independent-review-incidents-christmas-island-villawood-full.pdf.

21. Australian Human Rights Commission (2013). *Tell me about Enhanced screening*, https://www.humanrights.gov.au/our-work/asylum-seekers-and-refugees/publications/tell-me-about-enhanced-screening-process.
22. Law Council of Australia asylum seeker policy (2014), https://www.lawcouncil.asn.au/lawcouncil/images/LCA-PDF/a-z docs/AsylumSeeker_Policy_web.pdf.
23. Sanggaran, JP (2013). *Christmas Island Medical Officer's Letter of Concern: International Health and Medical services*, http://www.rch.org.au/uploadedFiles/Main/Content/immigranthealth/Xmas%20Island%20-%20letter-of-concern.pdf.
24. Australian Human Rights Commission (2014). *The Forgotten Children: National Inquiry into Children in Immigration Detention*, https://www.humanrights.gov.au/our-work/asylum-seekers-and-refugees/publications/forgotten-children-national-inquiry-children.
25. Moss, P. (2015). *Review into recent allegations relating to conditions and circumstances at the Regional Processing Centre in Nauru*, https://www.border.gov.au/ReportsandPublications/Documents/reviews-and-inquiries/review-conditions-circumstances-nauru.pdf.
26. The Coalition's Policy for a regional deterrence framework to combat people smuggling (2013), http://www.rowanramsey.com.au/Portals/0/PeopleSmuggling.pdf.
27. Law Council of Australia (2013). *Rule of law concerns over Migration Act changes*, http://www.lawcouncil.asn.au/lawcouncil/index.php/law-council-media/news/322-ruleoflawarticle.
28. Saul, B. (2012). Dark Justice: Australia's Indefinite Detention on Security Grounds under International Human Rights Law, http://law.unimelb.edu.au/__data/assets/pdf_file/0007/1687381/Saul.pdf.
29. Parliament of Australia (2014). *Migration and Maritime Powers*

Legislation Amendment (Resolving the Asylum Legacy Caseload) Bill, http://www.aph.gov.au/Parliamentary_Business/Bills_Legislation/Bills_Search_Results/Result?bId=r5346.

30. Shire, Warsan. *Home*. Headspace Press. 3 September 2016. http://headspacepress.com/home-by-warsan-shire/.

Acknowledgments

Enormous thanks to my beautiful and sassy Isabella Marie Rose, forced to endure the past four years sharing her mother with all things bookish, when really what she needed was Mum.

A massive thank you to John Holton writer/editor Burren Publications, this book could not have been written without the support and encouragement I received from John. He was the person I contacted when I had written the first 10,000 words to ask if it was worth me proceeding, he said *just keep writing, don't stop*, his words of encouragement made sure that's exactly what I did. John generously helped with editing and guiding my work in the early days and recently when brainstorming sub-title ideas, I will be forever grateful for his time, wisdom and general awesomeness.

Thank you to my big sister Marie-Therese who has been an incredible help with structural editing and offering advice and support along this journey. Anyone who says you shouldn't use your family to receive an honest critique of your work hasn't met my sister.

Huge thanks to Liz Graco my fabulous friend who always comes though with the goods. A talented photographer, Liz captured the images used for the book cover and marketing, thank you dear Liz.

Immense love and thanks to my parents Frank and Bernadette for always loving and supporting me, and for instilling the strong values of compassion and empathy.

My darling Hani, thank you for honouring me with your story and for your gift of abundance in living.

Heartfelt thanks to my dear colleagues from Christmas Island, Poh Lin Lee, Petrina Yates, Jan Wetzel, Leigh Johnston, Kerrie Berardi, Sean Devine, Kathryn Parle, Emma Swart, Jackie Fidler, Laurie Haynes, and Claire Voss you made the hard work we delivered that bit easier with shared passion, professionalism and kindness.

To my publisher Nick Walker for taking a chance with my book and to the publishing team at Australian Scholarly Publishing led by assistant editor Anastasia Buryak for bringing it all together, thank you.

Finally all my love and best wishes to those that inspired the book, Omid, Mohsen, Mustabja, Hani, Sabrin, Kafiya, Fatemeh, Zamen, Rohullah, Zahir, Mazen, Hussein, Raj, Mokhalad, Nahid, Udaya, Ahmed, Mohammad, Abbas, Sara, Nathan, Jude and Hayuran.

About the Author

Kerrie Wyatt Photography

Christine Cummins spent five years on Christmas Island as a Torture & Trauma counsellor working with asylum seekers detained in the immigration detention centre. She witnessed the arrival of thousands of men, women and children by boat and provided counselling and support to hundreds. Christine is a Credentialed Mental Health Nurse with a Masters in Mental Health; she is currently working as a Psychiatric Nurse Consultant. Christine has a background in social justice and human rights having worked with aid agencies in Sri Lanka and Iran and in the remote Kimberley region of Western Australia with indigenous communities. Christine is passionate about the need to maintain human dignity and access to basic human rights for all.

Printed in Australia
AUHW011207090519
311994AU00003B/10

9 781925 801569